The Spirit
of the
Liturgy

The Spirit of the Liturgy

ROMANO GUARDINI

Translated by
ADA LANE

Introduction by
JOANNE M. PIERCE

A Herder & Herder Book
The Crossroad Publishing Company
New York

The Crossroad Publishing Company
www.CrossroadPublishing.com

Original title *Vom Geist der Liturgie*
20th edition © 1997 Matthias-Grünewald,
Mainz/Ferdinand Schöningh, Paderborn

English translation was first published
in 1930 by Sheed & Ward in London

Introduction copyright © 1998 by Joanne M. Pierce

NIHIL OBSTAT GEORGIUS D SMITH, S T D, CENSOR DEPUTATUS

IMPRIMATUR EDM CAN SURMONT VIC GEN

WESTMONASTERII, DIE 13 OCTOBRIS 1930

Printed in the United States of America

Library of Congress Cataloging-in-Publication Data

Guardini, Romano, 1885-1968
    [Vom Geist der Liturgie   English]
    The spirit of the liturgy / Romano Guardini , translated by Ada Lane ,
introduction by Joanne M Pierce
        p   cm
    "A Herder & Herder book "
    Includes bibliographical references
    ISBN 0-8245-1777-6 (pbk)
    1 Catholic Church--Liturgy--Theology   I Title
BX1970 G7713   1998   98-20759
264' 02--dc21   CIP

This printing March 2016

CONTENTS

INTRODUCTION

THE AUTHOR

One of the most influential leaders of the liturgical movement in the first half of this century was Romano Guardini (1885-1968). An Italian by birth, Guardini spent most of his childhood in Germany, where his businessman father moved the family in 1886; as an adult, he continued his university education at several institutions in that country, moving from the fields of chemistry to economics to theology, and settling eventually at the University of Tübingen. After much painful soul-searching (including struggles with depression that would continue to trouble him throughout his life), Guardini finally decided to study for the Roman Catholic priesthood in his family's hometown of Mainz. He was ordained in 1910, and became a German citizen in 1911; after earning a Ph.D. in theology in 1915, he spent five years doing pastoral work and (during World War I) hospital service. In 1920, Guardini began work on his *Habilitationschrift*, the second dissertation that marks the final step in preparing for a German professorship; after its completion, he spent the majority of his life as a university professor, first at the Friedrich Wilhelm (now Humbolt) University in Berlin (1923-1939, until the Nazis forced his dismissal), then at the University of Munich (1948-1968).[1]

---

[1] These bibliographical details were drawn largely from Robert A. Krieg, C.S.C., "A Precursor's Life and Work," in Robert A. Krieg, C.S.C., ed., *Romano Guardini Proclaiming the Sacred in a Modern World* (Chicago: Liturgy Training Publications, 1995), pp. 15-29, esp. pp. 17-25. Some material was taken from Regina Kuehn, "Romano Guardini: The Teacher of Teachers," in Robert Tuzik, ed., *How Firm a Foundation Leaders of the Liturgical Movement* (Chicago: Liturgy Training Publications, 1990), pp. 36-49.

Guardini's life and work expanded far beyond the classrooms and libraries of universities. He spent five years at the beginning of his priestly career in pastoral ministry, where he began his decades-long involvement in youth ministry with the diocesan youth organization *Iuventus*. He continued to work with Catholic youth groups (including the Quickborn) during his time in Berlin,[2] and showed a special interest in women's issues (including service on the editorial board of a publication for young women, *Der neue Ring*).[3] Preaching was also a key component of his ministry, and had an important impact on the style and content of his written work.[4]

THE TEXT

One of his first publications, composed during that brief period of pastoral and hospital service during World War I,[5] was this short volume, *The Spirit of the Liturgy*, originally published in German in 1918, and in English translation in 1930. Even at the beginning of his career, Guardini had been influenced by some of the earliest figures of the liturgical movement in Europe. It was at the invitation of one of these, Abbot Ildefons Herwegen (1874-1946) of the abbey of Maria Laach, that this short book appeared as the first volume in the abbey's *Ecclesia Orans* series before Guardini had even finished his preparation for university teaching.

[2] Krieg, "A Precursor's Life and Work," pp. 20-23.

[3] Teresa Berger, "The Classical Liturgical Movement in Germany and Austria: Moved by Women?" *Worship* 66 (3/1993): 231-251; here, pp. 235-236.

[4] Guardini preached at the St. Benedict Chapel (known as the Students' Chapel) in Berlin and at the St. Ludwig Church at the University of Munich, among others. See Heinz R. Kuehn, "Fires in the Night: Germany 1920-1950," in Krieg, ed., *Romano Guardini*, pp. 1-14, here, pp. 6-8; and Krieg, "A Precursor's Life and Work," p. 25.

[5] According to Krieg, "A Precursor's Life and Work," pp. 20-21; Kuehn puts its composition during his student years at Tübingen; see Kuehn, "Romano Guardini," p. 38.

The abbey of Maria Laach was one of several great Benedictine centers of liturgical study in Europe; in addition to Abbot Herwegen, another of its monks, the renowned Odo Casel (1886-1948), would be one of Guardini's contemporaries and colleagues in the field of liturgics.[6]

The Spirit of the Liturgy was the first book published by Guardini. As an early fruit of his lifelong study of and reflection on the liturgy of the church, it is a key document in understanding the growth of his later writings. To some contemporary readers, Guardini's language may seem to echo a style of theological reflection that appears quaint, at best. However, Guardini's thought here must be more carefully considered. This influential volume is in fact a remarkable synthesis of several theological themes that would inform not only the later work of Pope Pius XII in *Mystici Corporis* (1943) and his great encyclical on the liturgy, *Mediator Dei* (1947), but also the groundbreaking documents of the Second Vatican Council (1962-1965), which themselves sparked the great liturgical reforms of the next two decades, not only in the Roman Catholic Church, but also in many other Christian churches.

The text of *The Spirit of the Liturgy* is divided into seven short chapters: "The Prayer of the Liturgy," "The Fellowship of the Liturgy," "The Style of the Liturgy," "The Symbolism of the Liturgy," "The Playfulness of the Liturgy," "The Seriousness of the Liturgy," and "The Primacy of the Logos over the Ethos." While the chapter titles do provide some clue as to the direction of Guardini's thought, they do not reveal the essence of his own "style." This is not an esoteric or technical book written for specialists, although Guardini does use sophisticated and "cutting edge" terminology and argument. His writing style, rather, is pitched in a more reflective mode,

---

[6] He and Guardini coedited the *Handbuch für Liturgiewissenschaft*; see "Odo Casel," in Kathleen Hughes, R.S.C.J., ed., *How Firm a Foundation Voices of the Early Liturgical Movement* (Chicago: Liturgy Training Publications, 1990), p. 69.

with a fluidity and concreteness of expression that makes his theology accessible to any thoughtful Catholic (or Christian) reader.

In order to appreciate Guardini's text, the post-conciliar reader must first place this book in the context of its original setting. During these early decades of the twentieth century, the theological movement known as Modernism was perceived as a formidable threat by the Catholic hierarchy. Guardini himself had been suspected of "Modernist" tendencies as a seminarian, and his ordination had been delayed by six months due to these suspicions.[7] The reader will note that, from the very beginning and throughout the text, Guardini is most careful to distance his thought on the nature of the liturgy from any Modernist tendencies.[8] His insistence on the permanent, "objective" and "eternal" character of liturgy (and of Christian doctrine in general) is a clear reaction against the more "evolutionary" models proposed by some of these thinkers. Guardini does not ignore the role of human culture in "shaping" the liturgy, however; he tries rather to contrast the "durable form" of the liturgy against more transitory and individual theological/ devotional expressions carried by "short waves of enthusiasm" (ch. 1). Indeed, the relationship between liturgy (faith) and culture would be one that Guardini would stress in much of his writing, and one that would eventually inform many of the documents of the Second Vatican Council.[9]

Additionally, Guardini's concept of the liturgy is clearly a corporate one. From the beginning of the book, and especially in the first two chapters, he stresses the "living unity" of the Church, the Body of Christ, which "celebrates" the liturgy (ch. 2); the Church

[7] Krieg, "A Precursor's Life and Work," pp. 19-20.

[8] Guardini's insistence on the decision-making role of the hierarchy is another example of the care he takes in guarding against any suggestion that historical or cultural context is the only determining factor of evaluating the validity of doctrine or practice.

[9] See Arno Schilson, "The Major Theological Themes of Romano Guardini," in Krieg, ed., *Romano Guardini*, pp. 31-42; here, pp. 34-37.

is a "liturgical entity" that "infinitely outnumbers the mere congregation" (ch. 1). The faithful are "actively united by a vital and fundamental principle . . . Christ himself; His life is ours; we are incorporated in Him; we are His Body, *Corpus Christi mysticum*" (ch. 2).

This corporate nature of the liturgy, with its strong Christological focus, counterbalances what Guardini sees as the "modern" (and "Protestant") focus on the independence of the individual.[10] The liturgy "requires" that the individual sacrifice self and live (and pray) with others in humility, a "breaking down of barriers" that, while careful and not "invasive," may still not come easily to the twentieth-century person (ch. 2). Here we see a related theme that would continue to occupy Guardini's thoughts: the influence of "modernity" on liturgical participation.[11] Guardini's line of thought here suggests another theological direction that he will address in part later in the volume, but that would bear richer fruit later in the century: the relationship between liturgical celebration and the call to do justice in the world.

Later chapters develop related themes. Guardini's short reflection on the "style" of the liturgy in chapter three continues to deal with the interrelationship between the "local" and the "universal" in the liturgy. Some of his remarks must be understood in context, since they refer more specifically to the shape and form of the Latin-language Tridentine liturgy of 1918, and to a wider theological debate about the interrelationship between the official liturgy of the Church and the various "private devotions" popular in various areas (addressed in *Mediator Dei* as well as by conciliar and post-conciliar documents). The deeper import of the tension between "particular" and "universal," however, is still pertinent in the con-

---

[10] See also Schilson, pp. 38-40.

[11] Kathleen Hughes, R.S.C.J., notes Guardini's continuing question: Are we capable of a genuine liturgical act? See Hughes, "Romano Guardini's View of Liturgy: A Lens for Our Time," in Krieg, ed., *Romano Guardini*, pp. 73-85; here, pp 74-79.

text of post-conciliar liturgical celebration, particularly in terms of his ongoing characterization of "modern man" and the difficulties of engaging in liturgical prayer. The Christocentric nature of the liturgy is again stressed, as is the organic unity of the Church as Body of Christ that provides the matrix of the "transcendence" of liturgical celebration. It is from personal "private devotion," however, that "liturgical prayer in its turn derives warmth and local color."

The next chapter deals with symbolism; in it Guardini articulates another important tension, one that will surface later in the century in wider theological discussion of the nature of symbol (and, of course, of liturgy). What is the connection, he asks, between the material and the spiritual? Guardini stresses the importance of the "bodily plane"; it cannot be disengaged or deleted in the quest for some "pure," non-corporeal spirituality. Neither, however, should the material be "inextricably jumbled together" with the spiritual; this, according to Guardini, leads to a misleading kind of projection of the individual emotional state, one that is always in a "state of flux."

Guardini's discussion of the "playfulness of the liturgy" (ch. 5) anticipates in many ways the classic analysis by Johan Huizinga in his *Homo ludens: A Study of the Play Element in Culture* (German, 1944; English, 1950). One key characteristic of the "play element" in liturgy emerges here: its essential purposelessness:[12] "the liturgy has no purpose, or, at least, it cannot be considered from the standpoint of purpose." Guardini links this "lack of purpose" first to the nature of the Triune God (the "delight" of the Father as Wisdom/Son "plays" before him, cf. Prv. 8: 30-31) and mystical "movement" before God, then to the aimless "play of the child," and finally to the creative expression of the artist.

---

[12] In fact, Huizinga cites Guardini's work in *The Spirit of the Liturgy* in his first chapter on the nature of play; see Huizinga, *Homo ludens A Study of the Play Element in Culture* (Boston: Beacon Press, 1955, 1967), p. 19.

Like play, however, "aimless" liturgy has its own seriousness, its own rules: "The liturgy has laid down the serious rules of the sacred game which the soul plays before God." The liturgical focus is the simplicity and mystery of existence before God, not "the restlessness of purposeful activity." Guardini's reflections on "wasting time" in liturgy have proved fruitful for several succeeding generations of liturgical theologians, as they have undertaken an analysis of the nature and essence of Christian ritual.

The notion of liturgy as play is counterbalanced in chapter six by reflections on the "seriousness of the liturgy." Here Guardini focuses on the beauty of the Church's liturgy, and the dangers of approaching it from a purely "aesthetic" point of view. The "power" of the Church and its liturgy is a "tool, used to carve the Kingdom of God from the raw material of the world," part of the "active life" of the Church. The "beauty" of the Church and its liturgy, part of its "contemplative side," derives from the very existence of the Church: art in the "process of transformation" into life. Guardini reiterates the scholastic maxim "Beauty is the splendor of truth" to stress the relationship between beauty and truth: "beauty is the triumphant splendor which breaks forth when the hidden truth is revealed, when the external phenomenon is at all points the perfect expression of the inner essence." It is this relationship that is missed by the aesthetic perspective, and that renders it ultimately "nerveless." Before the documents of Vatican II, before Pius XII, Guardini warned of the dangers of the superficiality of aestheticism in "appreciating" the liturgy. The real significance of the liturgy is salvation.

Guardini's final short chapter takes up once more the issue of modernity and the liturgy. Here he frames the discussion in terms of the contrast between certain dualities: knowledge and will, contemplative and active, Logos and Ethos. In this modern age, he states, it is will, Ethos, a preference for the active that have taken precedence over knowledge, Logos, and contemplation. Again in response to the challenges, not only of Protestant thought, but of

Modernism, Guardini criticizes the individualizing of truth, the tendency to "make conviction a matter of personal judgement, feeling, and experience," and to make truth "a relative and fluctuating value." Guardini is not attempting to break the connection between the liturgy (and thus the Church) and the world; in earlier chapters, he stresses the connection between liturgy (and the faith that informs it) and culture/civilization, as well as the connection between the spiritual and the bodily/material. Here he is instead highlighting the tendency for religion to become "cheerfully secular," concerned only with "time" and not directly or essentially with "eternity." Once again, Guardini stresses the Church's championing of "absolute truth" and the "tranquility" that it implies over the "restless" rootlessness of life "in continual flux . . . constant struggle, search, and wandering." This does not suggest that Logos is in some way "better" than Ethos, but rather that "in life as a whole, precedence does not belong to action, but to existence." It is in this more "existentialist" context that Guardini's repeated emphasis on the stillness, the reservedness, the "relaxation" and "reposefulness" of the liturgy must be understood.

CONCLUSION

Clearly, *The Spirit of the Liturgy* provides a remarkable synthesis of several key issues in twentieth-century liturgical theology. In addition to others of Guardini's books, for example, *The Church and the Catholic* (1935), *The Death of Socrates* (1948), *The Lord* (1954), *The End of the Modern World* (1956), and *The Wisdom of the Psalms* (1968), *The Spirit of the Liturgy* had a real impact on readers both in Europe and North America.[13] Full of important insights, the book retains its value for the contemporary reader. Of course, as Robert Krieg points out, there are certain parts of Guardini's text that are less relevant for postconciliar readers.

[13] See Robert A. Krieg, C.S.C., "North American Catholics' Reception of Romano Guardini's Writings," in Krieg, ed., *Romano Guardini*, pp. 43-59.

Guardini's original context is gone; the "pre-Vatican II Catholic 'world' no longer exists."[14] As advanced as his thinking was in the first decades of this century, the "theological horizon" has shifted in the years since the Council; some new issues (such as liturgical inculturation) have arisen, and other former issues (such as the tension between "private devotions" and "liturgy") have all but disappeared. This may make parts of Guardini's book seem, ironically, oddly conservative.[15] In all fairness to Guardini, however, one must not compartmentalize his insights along the lines of late twentieth-century theological/liturgical disputes.

As Kathleen Hughes notes, "These liturgists [of the liturgical movement] not only *lived* the liturgy but a remarkable number of them *died* liturgically."[16] Among the names of the great figures she lists should be found that of Romano Guardini. It is said that when news of his death on October 1, 1968, reached the ears of the members of the postconciliar commission on the implementation of the *Constitution on the Sacred Liturgy* then in session in Rome, they stood as one and chanted the *De profundis*.[17] His death, on what is now the feast day of St. Thérèse of Lisieux (recently named the third woman Doctor of the Church), marked the end of an era of preparation for liturgical reform, as well as the dawn of what many have called the "post-Vatican II world." Yet the epitaph on his Munich memorial stone speaks to the heart of both eras: "Believing in Jesus Christ and his Church/ Trusting in his merciful judgement."[18]

Joanne M. Pierce
College of the Holy Cross
Easter Week, 1998

---

[14] Krieg, "North American Catholics' Reception," p. 56.

[15] *Ibid.*

[16] Hughes, *How Firm a Foundation*, p. 6.

[17] Kuehn, "Romano Guardini," p. 36; cited by Krieg, "A Precursor's Life and Work," p. 27.

[18] Krieg, "A Precursor's Life and Work," p. 28.

Select Bibliography

Berger, Teresa. "The Classical Liturgical Movement in Germany and Austria: Moved by Women?" *Worship* 66 (3/1992): 231- 51.

Hughes, Kathleen, R.S.C.J., ed. *How Firm a Foundation: Voices of the Early Liturgical Movement*. Chicago: Liturgy Training Publications, 1990. (Contains selections from Guardini's writings, pp. 113-19.)

Huizinga, Johan. *Homo Ludens: A Study of the Play Element in Culture*. Boston: Beacon Press, 1955, 1967.

Krieg, Robert, C.S.C. *Romano Guardini: A Precursor of Vatican II*. Notre Dame, Ind.: University of Notre Dame Press, 1997.

Krieg, Robert, C.S.C., ed. *Romano Guardini: Proclaiming the Sacred in a Modern World*. Chicago: Liturgy Training Publications, 1995. (Contains several invaluable articles on Guardini's life, theology, and influence, in addition to a bibliography listing those of Guardini's works available in English, as well as English-language publications about Guardini.)

Kuehn, Heinz, ed. *The Essential Guardini: An Anthology of the Writings of Romano Guardini*. Chicago: Liturgy Training Publications, 1997.

Kuehn, Regina. "Romano Guardini: The Teacher of Teachers," in Robert Tuzik, ed., *How Firm a Foundation: Leaders of the Liturgical Movement*. Chicago: Liturgy Training Publications, 1990, pp. 36-49. (Contains entries on several of Guardini's contemporaries as well.)

THE PRAYER OF THE LITURGY

An old theological proverb says, "Nothing done by nature and grace is done in vain." Nature and grace obey their own laws, which are based upon certain established hypotheses. Both the natural and the supernatural life of the soul, when lived in accordance with these principles, remain healthy, develop, and are enriched. In isolated cases the rules may be waived without any danger, when such a course is required or excused by reason of a spiritual disturbance, imperative necessity, extraordinary occasion, important end in view, or the like. In the end, however, this cannot be done with impunity. Just as the life of the body droops and is stunted when the conditions of its growth are not observed, so it is with spiritual and religious life—it sickens, losing its vigor, strength and unity.

This is even more true where the regular spiritual life of a corporate body is concerned. Exceptions play a far greater part, after all, in the life of the individual than in that of the group. As soon as a group is in question, concern is immediately aroused with regard to the regulation of those practices and prayers which will constitute the permanent form of its devotion in common; and then the crucial question arises whether the fundamental laws which govern normal interior life—in the natural as in the supernatural order—are in this case to have currency or not. For it is no longer a question of the correct attitude to be adopted, from the spiritual point of view, towards the adjustment of some temporary requirement or need, but of the form to be taken by the permanent legislation which will henceforth exercise an enduring influence upon the soul. This is not intended to regulate entirely independent cases, each on its own merits, but to take into account the average requirements and demands of everyday life. It is not to serve as a model for the spiritual life of the individual, but for that of a corporate body, composed of the most distinct and varied elements. From this it follows that any defect in its organization will inevitably become both apparent and obtrusive. It is true that at first every mistake will be completely overshadowed by the particular circumstances—the emergency or disturbance—which justified the adoption of that particular line of conduct. But in proportion as the extraordinary symptoms subside, and the normal existence of the soul is resumed, the more forcibly every interior mistake is bound to come to light, sowing destruction on all sides in its course.

The fundamental conditions essential to the full expansion of spiritual life as it is lived in common are most clearly discernible in the devotional life of any great community which has spread its development over a long period of time. Its scheme of life has by then matured and developed its full value. In a corporate body—composed of people of highly varied circumstances, drawn from distinct social strata, perhaps even from different races, in the course of different historical and cultural periods—the ephemeral, adventitious, and locally characteristic elements are, to a certain extent, eliminated, and that which is universally accepted as binding and essential comes to the fore. In other words, the canon of spiritual administration becomes, in the course of time, objective and impartial.

The Catholic liturgy is the supreme example of an objectively established rule of spiritual life. It has been able to develop *kata ton holon,* that is to say, in every direction, and in accordance with all places, times, and types of human culture. Therefore it will be the best teacher of the *via ordinaria*—the regulation of religious life in common, with, at the same time, a view to actual needs and requirements.[1]

---

[1] It is not by chance that "the religious Pope" so resolutely took in hand the revision of the liturgy. The internal revival of the Catholic community will not

The significance of the liturgy must, however, be more exactly defined. Our first task will be to establish the quality of its relation to the non-liturgical forms of spiritual life.

The primary and exclusive aim of the liturgy is not the expression of the individual's reverence and worship for God. It is not even concerned with the awakening, formation, and sanctification of the individual soul as such. Nor does the onus of liturgical action and prayer rest with the individual. It does not even rest with the collective groups, composed of numerous individuals, who periodically achieve a limited and intermittent unity in their capacity as the congregation of a church. The liturgical entity consists rather of the united body of the faithful as such—the Church—a body which infinitely outnumbers the mere congregation. The liturgy is the Church's public and lawful act of worship, and it is performed and conducted by the officials whom the Church herself has designated for the post—her priests. In the liturgy God is to be honored by the body of the faithful, and the latter is in its turn to derive sanctification from this act of worship. It is important that this objective nature of the liturgy should be fully understood. Here the Catholic conception of worship in common sharply differs from the Protestant, which is predominantly individualistic. The fact that the individual Catholic, by his absorption into the higher unity, finds liberty and discipline, originates in the twofold nature of man, who is both social and solitary.

make progress until the liturgy again occupies its rightful position in Catholic life. And the Eucharistic movement can only effectually distribute its blessings when it is in close touch with the liturgy. It was the Pope who issued the Communion Decrees who also said, "You must not *pray* at Mass, you must *say* Mass!" Only when the Blessed Sacrament is understood from the point of view of the liturgy can It take that active share in the religious regeneration of the world which Pius X expected of It. (In the same way the full active and moral power of the Blessed Sacrament is only free to operate unchecked when Its connection with the problems and tasks of public and family life, and with those of Christian charity and of vocational occupations, is fully comprehended.)

Now, side by side with the strictly ritual and entirely objective forms of devotion, others exist, in which the personal element is more strongly marked. To this type belong those which are known as "popular devotions," such as afternoon prayers accompanied by hymns, devotions suited to varying periods, localities, or requirements, and so on. They bear the stamp of their time and surroundings, and are the direct expression of the characteristic quality or temper of an individual congregation.

Private piety

Although in comparison with the prayer of the individual, which is expressive of purely personal needs and aspirations, popular devotions are both communal and objective, they are to a far greater degree characteristic of their origin than is the liturgy, the entirely objective and impersonal method of prayer practiced by the Church as a whole. This is the reason for the greater stress laid by popular devotion upon the individual need of edification. Hence the rules and forms of liturgical practice cannot be taken, without more ado, as the authoritative and decisive standard for non-liturgical prayer. The claim that the liturgy should be taken as the exclusive pattern of devotional practice in common can never be upheld. To do so would be to confess complete ignorance of the spiritual requirements of the greater part of the faithful. The forms of popular piety should rather continue to exist side by side with those of the liturgy, and should constitute themselves according to the varying requirements of historical, social, and local conditions. There could be no greater mistake than that of discarding the valuable elements in the spiritual life of the people for the sake of the liturgy, or than the desire of assimilating them to it. But in spite of the fact that the liturgy and popular devotion have each their own special premises and aims, still it is to liturgical worship that preeminence of right belongs. The liturgy is and will be the *lex orandi.* Non-liturgical prayer must take the liturgy for its model, and must renew itself in the liturgy, if it is to retain its vitality. It cannot precisely be said that as dogma is to private religious opinion, so is the liturgy to liturgy correct devotion

popular devotion; but the connection between the latter does to a certain degree correspond with that special relation, characteristic of the former, which exists between the government and the governed. All other forms of devotional practice can always measure their shortcomings by the standard of the liturgy, and with its help find the surest way back to the *via ordinaria* when they have strayed from it. The changing demands of time, place, and special circumstance can express themselves in popular devotion; facing the latter stands the liturgy, from which clearly issue the fundamental laws—eternally and universally unchanging—which govern all genuine and healthy piety.

In the following pages an attempt will be made to select from the liturgy and to analyze several of these laws. But it is an attempt pure and simple, which professes to be neither exhaustive nor conclusive.

The first and most important lesson which the liturgy has to teach is that the prayer of a corporate body must be sustained by thought. The prayers of the liturgy are entirely governed by and interwoven with dogma. Those who are unfamiliar with liturgical prayer often regard them as theological formula, artistic and didactic, until on closer acquaintance they suddenly perceive and admit that the clear-cut, lucidly constructed phrases are full of interior enlightenment. To give an outstanding example, the wonderful Collects of the Masses of Sunday may be quoted. Wherever the stream of prayer wells abundantly upwards, it is always guided into safe channels by means of plain and lucid thought. Interspersed among the pages of the Missal and the Breviary are readings from Holy Scripture and from the works of the Fathers, which continually stimulate thought. Often these readings are introduced and concluded by short prayers of a characteristically contemplative and reflective nature—the antiphons—during which that which has been heard or read has time to cease echoing and to sink into the mind. The liturgy, the *lex orandi*, is, according to the old proverb, the law of faith—the *lex credendi*—as well. It is the treasure-house of the thought of Revelation.

This is not, of course, an attempt to deny that the heart and the emotions play an important part in the life of prayer. Prayer is, without a doubt, "a raising of the heart to God." But the heart must be guided, supported, and purified by the mind. In individual cases or on definite and explicit occasions it may be possible to persist in, and to derive benefit from, emotion pure and simple, either spontaneous or occasioned by a fortunate chance. But a regular and recurrent form of devotion lights upon the most varied moods, because no one day resembles another. If the content of these devotional forms is of a predominantly emotional character, it will bear the stamp of its fortuitous origin, since the feeling engendered by solitary spiritual occurrences flows for the most part into special and particular channels. Such a prayer therefore will always be unsuitable if it does not harmonize, to a certain degree at least, with the disposition of the person who is to offer it. Unless this condition is complied with, either it is useless or it may even mar the sentiment experienced. The same thing occurs when a form of prayer intended for a particular purpose is considered to be adapted to the most varied occasions.

Only thought is universally current and consistent, and, as long as it is really thought, remains suited, to a certain degree, to every intelligence. If prayer in common, therefore, is to prove beneficial to the majority, it must be primarily directed by thought, and not by feeling. It is only when prayer is sustained by and steeped in clear and fruitful religious thought, that it can be of service to a corporate body, composed of distinct elements, all actuated by varying emotions.

We have seen that thought alone can keep spiritual life sound and healthy. In the same way, prayer is beneficial only when it rests on the bedrock of truth. This is not meant in the purely negative sense that it must be free from error; in addition to this, it must spring from the fullness of truth. It is only truth—or dogma, to give it its other name—which can make prayer efficacious, and impregnate it with that austere, protective strength without which it degenerates into weakness. If this is true of private prayer, it is doubly so of popular devotion, which in many directions verges on sentimentality.[2] Dogmatic thought brings release from the thralldom of individual caprice, and from the uncertainty and sluggishness which follow in the wake of emotion. It makes prayer intelligible, and causes it to rank as a potent factor in life.

If, however, religious thought is to do justice to its mission, it must introduce into prayer truth in all its fullness.

Various individual truths of Revelation hold a special attraction for the temperaments and conditions to which they correspond. It is easy to see that certain people have a pronounced predilection for certain mysteries of faith. This is shown in the case of converts, for instance, by the religious ideas which first arrested their attention at their entry into the Church, or which decided them on the step they were taking, and in other cases by the truths which at the approach of doubt form the mainstay and buttress of the whole house of faith. In the same way doubt does not charge at random, but attacks for the most part those mysteries of faith which appeal least to the temperament of the people concerned.[3]

If a prayer therefore stresses any one mystery of faith in an exclusive or an excessive manner, in the end it will adequately

---

[2] A proof of this is to be found in the often sugary productions of sacred art—holy pictures, statues, etc.—which appeal to the people. The people are susceptible to powerful art when it is national; the Middle Ages are a witness to this, and certain aspects of modern art. But the danger of lapsing into mere insipidity is very great. The same thing applies to popular songs, and holds good in other directions as well.

[3] This does not mean that these truths are merely a mental indication of the existing spiritual condition of the person concerned. It is rather a proof of the saying, "grace takes nature for granted." Revelation finds in a man's natural turn of mind the necessary spiritual premises by which the truths, which are of themselves mysteries, can be more easily grasped and adhered to.

satisfy none but those who are of a corresponding temperament, and even the latter will eventually become conscious of their need of truth in its entirety. For instance, if a prayer deals exclusively with God's mercy, it will not ultimately satisfy even a delicate and tender piety, because this truth calls for its complement—the fact of God's justice and majesty. In any form of prayer, therefore, which is intended for the ultimate use of a corporate body, the whole fullness of religious truth must be included.

Here, too, the liturgy is our teacher. It condenses into prayer the entire body of religious truth. Indeed, it is nothing else but truth expressed in terms of prayer. For it is the great fundamental truths[4] which above all fill the liturgy—God in His mighty reality, perfection, and greatness, One, and Three in One; His creation, providence, and omnipresence; sin, justification, and the desire of salvation; the Redeemer and His kingdom; the four last things. It is only such an overwhelming abundance of truth which can never pall, but continue to be, day after day, all things to all men, ever fresh and inexhaustible.

In the end, therefore, prayer in common will be fruitful only in so far as it does not concentrate markedly, or at any rate exclusively, on particular portions of revealed truth, but embraces, as far as possible, the whole of Divine teaching. This is especially important where the people are concerned, because they easily tend to develop a partiality for particular mysteries of faith which for some reason have become dear to them.[5] On the other hand, it is

---

[4] It is a further proof of Pius X's perspicacity that he made universally accessible precisely those portions of the liturgy—Sundays, the weekly office, and especially the daily Masses of Lent—which stress the great fundamental mysteries of faith.

[5] By this we do not mean that specific times (e.g., the stress of war) and conditions (e.g., the special needs of an agricultural or seafaring population) do not bring home certain truths more vividly than others. We are dealing here with the universal principle, which is, however, adaptable and must make allowances for special cases.

obvious that prayer must not be overladen and as a result form a mere hotchpotch of ill-assorted thoughts and ideas—a thing which sometimes does occur. Yet without the element of spaciousness, spiritual life droops and becomes narrow and petty. "The truth shall make you free"—free not only from the thralldom of error, but free as a preparation for the vastness of God's kingdom.

While the necessity of thought is emphasized, it must not be allowed to degenerate into the mere frigid domination of reason. Devotional forms on the contrary should be permeated by warmth of feeling.

On this point as well the liturgy has many recommendations to make. The ideas which fill it are vital: that is to say, they spring from the impulses of the heart which has been molded by grace, and must again in their turn affect other eager and ardent hearts. The Church's worship is full of deep feeling, of emotion that is intense, and sometimes even vehement. Take the Psalms, for instance—how deeply moving they often are! Listen to the expression of longing in the *Quemadmodum*, of remorse in the *Miserere*, of exultation in the Psalms of praise, and of indignant righteousness in those denouncing the wicked. Or consider the remarkable spiritual tension which lies between the mourning of Good Friday and the joy of Easter morning.

Liturgical emotion is, however, exceedingly instructive. It has its moments of supreme climax, in which all bounds are broken, as, for instance, in the limitless rejoicing of the *Exultet* on Holy Saturday. But as a rule it is controlled and subdued. The heart speaks powerfully, but thought at once takes the lead; the forms of prayer are elaborately constructed, the constituent parts carefully counterbalanced; and as a rule they deliberately keep emotion under strict control. In this way, in spite of the deep feeling to be found in, say, the Psalms (to instance them once more), a sense of restraint pervades liturgical form.

The liturgy as a whole is not favorable to exuberance of feeling. Emotion glows in its depths, but it smolders merely, like the fiery heart of the volcano, whose summit stands out clear and serene against the quiet sky. The liturgy *is* emotion, but it is emotion under the strictest control. We are made particularly aware of this at Holy Mass, and it applies equally to the prayers of the Ordinary and of the Canon, and to those of the Proper of the Time. Among them are to be found masterpieces of spiritual restraint.

The restraint characteristic of the liturgy is at times very pronounced—so much so as to make this form of prayer appear at first as a frigid intellectual production, until we gradually grow familiar with it and realize what vitality pulsates in the clear, measured forms.

And how necessary this discipline is! At certain moments and on certain occasions it is permissible for emotion to have a vent. But a prayer which is intended for the everyday use of a large body of people must be restrained. If, therefore, it has uncontrolled and unbalanced emotion for a foundation, it is doubly dangerous. It will operate in one of two ways. Either the people who use it will take it seriously, and probably will then feel obliged to force themselves into acquiescence with an emotion that they have never, generally speaking, experienced, or which, at any rate, they are not experiencing at that particular moment, thus perverting and degrading their religious feeling. Or else indifference, if they are of a phlegmatic temperament, will come to their aid; they then take the phrases at less than their face value, and consequently the word is depreciated.

Written prayer is certainly intended as a means of instruction and of promoting an increased sensibility. But its remoteness from the average emotional attitude must not be allowed to become too great. If prayer is ultimately to be fruitful and beneficial to a corporate body, it must be intense and profound, but at the same time

normally tranquil in tone. The wonderful verses of the hymn—
hardly translatable, so full are they of penetrating insight—may be
quoted in this connection:

> *Laeti bibamus sobriam*
> *Ebrietatem Spiritus . . .*[6]

Certainly we must not try to measure off the lawful share of
emotion with a foot-rule; but where a plain and straightforward
expression suffices we must not aggrandize nor embellish it; and a
simple method of speech is always to be preferred to an overloaded
one.

Again, the liturgy has many suggestions to make on the quality of the emotion required for the particular form of prayer under
discussion, which is ultimately to prove universally beneficial. It
must not be too choice in expression, nor spring from special sec-
tions of dogma, but clearly express the great fundamental feelings,
both natural and spiritual, as do the Psalms, for instance, where we
find the utterance of adoration, longing for God, gratitude, suppli-
cation, awe, remorse, love, readiness for sacrifice, courage in suf-
fering, faith, confidence, and so on. The emotion must not be too
acutely penetrating, too tender, or too delicate, but strong, clear,
simple and natural.

Then the liturgy is wonderfully reserved. It scarcely expresses,
even, certain aspects of spiritual surrender and submission, or else
it veils them in such rich imagery that the soul still feels that it is
hidden and secure. The prayer of the Church does not probe and
lay bare the heart's secrets; it is as restrained in thought as in imagery; it does, it is true, awaken very profound and very tender emotions and impulses, but it leaves them hidden. There are certain
feelings of surrender, certain aspects of interior candor which cannot be publicly proclaimed, at any rate in their entirety, without
danger to spiritual modesty. The liturgy has perfected a masterly

---

[6] From the Benedictine Breviary, Lauds (i.e., the prayer at daybreak) of Tues-
day. [Literally, "Let us joyfully taste of the sober drunkenness of the Spirit."]

instrument which has made it possible for us to express our inner
life in all its fullness and depth, without divulging our secrets—
secretum meum mihi. We can pour out our hearts, and still feel that
nothing has been dragged to light that should remain hidden.[7]

This is equally true of the system of moral conduct which is to
be found in prayer.

Liturgical action and liturgical prayer are the logical consequences of certain moral premises—the desire for justification,
contrition, readiness for sacrifice, and so on—and often issue afresh
into moral actions. But there again it is possible to observe a fine
distinction. The liturgy does not lightly exact moral actions of a
very far-reaching nature, especially those which denote an interior
decision. It requires them where the matter is of real importance,
e.g., the abjuration at baptism, or the vows at the final reception
into an order. When, however, it is a question of making regular
daily prayer fruitful in everyday intentions and decisions, the liturgy is very cautious. For instance, it does not rashly utter such
things as vows, or full and permanent repudiations of sin, entire
and lasting surrender, all-embracing consecration of one's entire
being, utter contempt for and renouncement of the world, prom-
ises of exclusive love, and the like. Such ideas are present at times,
fairly frequently even, but generally under the form of a humble
entreaty that the suppliant may be vouchsafed similar sentiments,
or that he is encouraged to ponder upon their goodness and nobil-

---

[7] The liturgy here accomplishes on the spiritual plane what has been done on
the temporal by the dignified forms of social intercourse, the outcome of the
tradition created and handed down by sensitive people. This makes communal
life possible for the individual, and yet insures him against unauthorized interfer-
ence with his inner self; he can be cordial without sacrificing his spiritual independence, he is in communication with his neighbor without on that account being swallowed up and lost among the crowd. In the same way the liturgy preserves freedom of spiritual movement for the soul by means of a wonderful union
of spontaneity and the finest erudition. It extols *urbanitas* as the best antidote to
barbarism, which triumphs when spontaneity and culture alike are no more.

ity, or is exhorted on the same subject. But the liturgy avoids the frequent use of those prayers in which these moral actions are specifically expressed.

How right this is! In moments of exaltation and in the hour of decision such a manner of speech may be justified, and even necessary. But when it is a question of the daily spiritual life of a corporate body, such formulas, when frequently repeated, offer those who are using them an unfortunate selection from which to make their choice. Perhaps they take the formulas literally and endeavor to kindle the moral sentiments expressed in them, discovering later that it is often difficult, and sometimes impossible, to do so truthfully and effectually. They are consequently in danger of developing artificial sentiments, of forcing intentions that still remain beyond their compass, and of daily performing moral actions, which of their very nature cannot be frequently accomplished. Or else they take the words merely as a passing recommendation of a line of conduct which it would be well to adopt, and in this way depreciate the intrinsic moral value of the formula, although it may be used frequently, and in all good faith. In this connection are applicable the words of Christ, "Let your speech be yea, yea,—nay, nay."[8]

The liturgy has solved the problem of providing a constant incentive to the highest moral aims, and at the same time of remaining true and lofty, while satisfying everyday needs.

Another question which arises is that concerning the form to be taken by prayer in common. We may put it like this: What method of prayer is capable of transforming the souls of a great multitude of people, and of making this transformation permanent?

The model of all devotional practice in common is to be found in the Divine Office, which day after day gathers together great bodies of people at stated times for a particular purpose. If anywhere, then it is in the Office that those conditions will be found

[8] Matt. v. 37.

which are favorable to the framing of rules for the forms of prayer in common.[9]

It is of paramount importance that the whole gathering should take an active share in the proceedings. If those composing the gathering merely listen, while one of the number acts as spokesman, the interior movement soon stagnates. All present, therefore, are obliged to take part. It is not even sufficient for the gathering to do so by repeating the words of their leader. This type of prayer does, of course, find a place in the liturgy, e.g., in the litany. It is perfectly legitimate, and people desirous of abandoning it totally fail to recognize the requirements of the human soul. In the litany the congregation answers the varying invocations of the leader with an identical act, e.g., with a request. In this way the act each time acquires a fresh content and fresh fervor, and an intensification of ardor is the result. It is a method better suited than any other to express a strong, urgent desire, or a surrender to God's Will, presenting as it does the petition of all sides effectively and simultaneously.

But the liturgy does not employ this method of prayer frequently; we may even say, when we consider divine worship as a whole, that it employs it but seldom. And rightly so, for it is a method which runs the risk of numbing and paralyzing spiritual movement.[10] The liturgy adapts the dramatic form by choice to the

---

[9] We do not overlook the fact that the Office in its turn presupposes its special relations and conditions, from which useful hints may be gained for private devotion, such as the necessity for a great deal of leisure, which enables the soul to meditate more deeply; and a special erudition, which opens the mind to the world of ideas and to artistry of form, and so on.

[10] The foregoing remarks on the liturgy have already made it abundantly clear that the justification of methods of prayer such as, e.g., the Rosary, must not be gainsaid. They have a necessary and peculiar effect in the spiritual life. They clearly express the difference which exists between liturgical and popular prayer. The liturgy has for its fundamental principle, *Ne bis idem* [there must be no repetition]. It aims at a continuous progress of ideas, mood and intention. Popular devotion, on the contrary, has a strongly contemplative character, and loves to

fundamental requirements of prayer in common. It divides those
present into two choirs, and causes prayer to progress by means of
dialogue. In this way all present join the proceedings, and are
obliged to follow with a certain amount of attention at least, know-
ing as they do that the continuation of their combined action depends upon each one personally.

Here the liturgy lays down one of the fundamental principles
of prayer, which cannot be neglected with impunity.[11] However
justified the purely responsive forms of prayer may be, the primary form of prayer in common is the actively progressive—that
much we learn from the *lex orandi*. And the question, intensely
important today, as to the right method to employ in again winning
people to the life of the Church is most closely connected with the
question under discussion. For it is modern people precisely who
insist upon vital and progressive movement, and an active share in
things. The fluid mass of this overwhelming spiritual material, however, needs cutting down and fashioning. It requires a leader to
regulate the beginning, omissions, and end, and, in addition, to
organize the external procedure. The leader also has to model it
interiorly; thus, for instance, he has to introduce the recurrent
thought-theme, himself undertaking the harder portions, in order
that they may be adequately and conscientiously dealt with; he

linger around a few simple images, ideas and moods without any swift changes of
thought. For the people the forms of devotion are often merely a means of being
with God. On this account they love repetition. The ever-renewed requests of the
Our Father, Hail Mary, etc. are for them at the same time receptacles into which
they can pour their hearts.

[11] In earlier ages the Church practiced by preference the so called "responsive" form of chanting the Psalms. The Precentor chanted one verse after the
other, and the people answered with the identical verse, or the partially repeated
verse. But at the same time another method was in use, according to which the
people divided into two choirs, and each alternately chanted a verse of the Psalm.
It says much for the sureness of liturgical instinct that the second method entirely
supplanted the first. (Cf. Thalhofer-Eisenhofer, "Handbuch der katholischen
Liturgik," Freiburg, 1902, I, 261 et seq.)

must express the emotion of all present by means of climaxes, and introduce certain restful pauses by the inclusion of didactic or meditative portions. Such is the task of the choir-leader, which has undergone a carefully graduated course of development in the liturgy.

Attention has already been called to the deep and fruitful emotion which is contained in the liturgy. It also embraces the two fundamental forces of human existence: Nature and civilization.

In the liturgy the voice of Nature makes itself heard clearly and decisively. We only need to read the Psalms to see man as he really is. There the soul is shown as courageous and despondent, happy and sorrowful, full of noble intentions, but of sin and struggles as well, zealous for everything that is good and then again apathetic and dejected. Or let us take the readings from the Old Testament. How frankly human nature is revealed in them! There is no attempt at extenuation or excuse. The same thing applies to the Church's words of ordination, and to the prayers used in administering the sacraments. A truly refreshing spontaneity characterizes them; they call things by their names. Man is full of weakness and error, and the liturgy acknowledges this. Human nature is inexplicable, a tangled web of splendor and misery, of greatness and baseness, and as such it appears in the prayer of the Church. Here we find no carefully adapted portrait from which the harsh and unpleasing traits have been excluded, but man as he is.

Not less rich is the liturgy's cultural heritage. We become conscious of the fact that many centuries have cooperated in its formation and have bequeathed to it of their best. They have fashioned its language; expanded its ideas and conceptions in every direction; developed its beauty of construction down to the smallest detail—the short verses and the finely-forged links of the prayers, the artistic form of the Divine Office and of the Mass, and the wonderful whole that is the ecclesiastical year. Action, narrative, and choral forms combine to produce the cumulative effect. The style of the individual forms continually varies—simple and clear in the Hours, rich in mystery on the festivals of Mary, resplendent on the more modern feasts, delightful and full of charm in the offices of the early virgin-martyrs. To this we should add the entire group of ritual gestures and action, the liturgical vessels and vestments, and the works of sculptors and artists and musicians.

In all this is to be learned a really important lesson on liturgical practice. Religion needs civilization. By civilization we mean the essence of the most valuable products of man's creative, constructive, and organizing powers—works of art, science, social orders, and the like. In the liturgy it is civilization's task to give durable form and expression to the treasure of truths, aims, and supernatural activity, which God has delivered to man by Revelation, to distill its quintessence, and to relate this to life in all its multiplicity. Civilization is incapable of creating a religion, but it can supply the latter with a *modus operandi*, so that it can freely engage in its beneficent activity. That is the real meaning of the old proverb, *Philosophia ancilla theologiae*—philosophy is the handmaid of theology. It applies to all the products of civilization, and the Church has always acted in accordance with it. Thus she knew very well what she was doing, for instance, when she absolutely obliged the Order of Saint Francis—brimming over with high aspirations, and spiritual energy and initiative—to adopt a certain standard of living, property, learning, and so on. Only a prejudiced mind, with no conception of the fundamental conditions essential to normal spiritual life, would see in this any deterioration of the first high aims. By her action in the matter the Church, on the contrary, prepared the ground for the Order, so that in the end it could remain healthy and productive. Individuals, or short waves of enthusiasm, can to a wide degree dispense with learning and culture. This is proved by the beginnings of the desert Orders in Egypt, and of the mendicant friars, and by holy people in all ages. But, generally speaking, a fairly high degree of genuine learning and culture is necessary in the long run, in order to keep spiritual life healthy. By means of these two things spiritual life retains its energy, clearness, and catholicity. Culture preserves spiritual life from the unhealthy, eccentric, and one-sided elements with which it tends to get involved only too easily. Culture enables religion to express itself, and helps it to distinguish what is essential from what is nonessential, the means from the end, and the path from the goal. The Church has always condemned every attempt at attacking science, art, property, and so on. The same Church which so resolutely stresses the "one thing necessary," and which upholds with the greatest impressiveness the teaching of the Evangelical Counsels—that we must be ready to sacrifice everything for the sake of eternal salvation—nevertheless desires, as a rule, that spiritual life should be impregnated with the wholesome salt of genuine and lofty culture.

But spiritual life is in precisely as great a need of the subsoil of healthy nature—"grace takes nature for granted." The Church has clearly shown her views on the subject by the gigantic struggles waged against Gnosticism and Manichaeism, against the Catharists and the Albigenses, against Jansenism and every kind of fanaticism. This was done by the same Church which, in the face of Pelagius and Celestius, of Jovinian and Helvidius, and of the immoderate exaltation of nature, powerfully affirmed the existence of grace and of the supernatural order, and asserted that the Christian must overcome nature. The lack of fruitful and lofty culture causes spiritual life to grow numbed and narrow; the lack of the subsoil of healthy nature makes it develop on mawkish, perverted, and unfruitful lines. If the cultural element of prayer declines, the ideas become impoverished, the language coarse, the imagery clumsy and monotonous; in the same way, when the lifeblood of nature no longer flows vigorously in its veins, the ideas become empty and tedious, the emotion paltry and artificial, and the imagery lifeless and insipid. Both—the lack of natural vigor and the lack of lofty culture—together constitute what we call barbarism, i.e., the exact contradiction of that "*scientia vocis*" which is revealed in liturgical prayer and is reverenced by the liturgy itself as the sublime prerogative of the holy Creative Principle.[12]

Prayer must be simple, wholesome, and powerful. It must be closely related to actuality and not afraid to call things by their names. In prayer we must find our entire life over again. On the other hand, it must be rich in ideas and powerful images, and speak a developed but restrained language; its construction must be clear and obvious to the simple man, stimulating and refreshing to the man of culture. It must be intimately blended with an erudition which is in nowise obtrusive, but which is rooted in breadth of spiritual outlook and in inward restraint of thought, volition, and emotion.

And that is precisely the way in which the prayer of the liturgy has been formed.

[12] The above remarks must not be misunderstood. Certainly the grace of God is self-sufficient, neither nature nor the work of man is necessary in order that a soul may be sanctified. God "can awaken of these stones children to Abraham." But as a rule He wishes that everything which belongs to man in the way of good, lofty, natural and cultural possessions shall be placed at the disposal of religion and so serve the Kingdom of God. He has interconnected the natural and the supernatural order, and has given natural things a place in the scheme of His supernatural designs. It is the duty of his representative on earth, ecclesiastical authority, to decide how and to what extent these natural means of attaining the supernatural goal are to be utilized.

THE FELLOWSHIP OF THE LITURGY

The liturgy does not say "I," but "We," unless the particular action which is being performed specifically requires the singular number (e.g., a personal declaration, certain prayers offered by the bishop or the priest in his official capacity, and so on). The liturgy is not celebrated by the individual, but by the body of the faithful. This is not composed merely of the persons who may be present in church; it is not the assembled congregation. On the contrary, it reaches out beyond the bounds of space to embrace all the faithful on earth. Simultaneously it reaches beyond the bounds of time, to this extent, that the body which is praying upon earth knows itself to be at one with those for whom time no longer exists, who, being perfected, exist in Eternity.

Yet this definition does not exhaust the conception of the universality and the all-embracingness which characterize the fellowship of the liturgy. The entity which performs the liturgical actions is not merely the sum total of all individual Catholics. It does consist of all these united in one body, but only in so far as this unity is of itself something, apart from the millions which compose it. And that something is the Church.

Here we find an analogy with what happens in the body politic. The State is more than the sum total of citizens, authorities, laws, organizations, and so on. In this connection discussion of the time-honored question—whether this higher unity is real or imagined—is beside the point. In any case, as far as personal perception is concerned, it does exist. The members of a State are not only conscious of being parts of a greater whole, but also of being as it were members of an overlapping, fundamental, living unity.

On an essentially different plane—the supernatural—a more or less corresponding phenomenon may be witnessed in the Church.

The Church is self-contained, a structure-system of intricate and invisible vital principles, of means and ends, of activity and production, of people, organizations, and laws. It does consist of the faithful, then; but it is more than the mere body of these, passively held together by a system of similar convictions and regulations. The faithful are actively united by a vital and fundamental principle common to them all. That principle is Christ Himself; His life is ours; we are incorporated in Him; we are His Body, *Corpus Christi mysticum.*[13] The active force which governs this living unity, grafting the individual on to it, granting him a share in its fellowship and preserving this right for him, is the Holy Ghost.[14] Every individual Catholic is a cell of this living organism or a member of this Body.

The individual is made aware of the unity which comprehends him on many and various occasions, but chiefly in the liturgy. In it he sees himself face to face with God, not as an entity, but as a member of this unity. It is the unity which addresses God; the individual merely speaks in it, and it requires of him that he should know and acknowledge that he is a member of it.

It is on the plane of liturgical relations that the individual experiences the meaning of religious fellowship. The individual— provided that he actually desires to take part in the celebration of the liturgy—must realize that it is as a member of the Church that he, and the Church within him, acts and prays; he must know that in this higher unity he is at one with the rest of the faithful, and he must desire to be so.

From this, however, arises a very perceptible difficulty. It is chiefly to be traced to a more common one, concerning the relation between the individual and the community. The religious com-

---

[13] Cf. Rom. xii. 4 et seq.; I Cor. xii. 4 et seq.; Eph., chaps. i.-iv.; Col. i. 15 et seq., and elsewhere.

[14] Cf I Cor. xii. 4 et seq.; M. J. Scheeben, "Die Mysterien des Christentums," pp. 314-508 (Freiburg, 1911).

munity, like every other, exacts two things from the individual. The first is a sacrifice, which consists in the renouncement by the individual of everything in him which exists merely for itself and excludes others, while and in so far as he is an active member of the community: he must lay self aside, and live with, and for, others, sacrificing to the community a proportion of his self-sufficiency and independence. In the second place he must produce something; and that something is the widened outlook resulting from his acceptance and assimilation of a more comprehensive scheme of life than his own—that of the community.

This demand will be differently met, according to the disposition of each individual. Perhaps it will be the more impersonal element of spiritual life—the ideas, the ordering of instruments and designs, the objectives, laws and rules, the tasks to be accomplished, the duties and rights, and so on—which first arrests the attention. Both the sacrifice and production indicated above will in such cases assume a more concrete character. The individual has to renounce his own ideas and his own way. He is obliged to subscribe to the ideas and to follow the lead of the liturgy. To it he must surrender his independence; pray with others, and not alone; obey, instead of freely disposing of himself; and stand in the ranks, instead of moving about at his own will and pleasure. It is, furthermore, the task of the individual to apprehend clearly the ideal world of the liturgy. He must shake off the narrow trammels of his own thought, and make his own a far more comprehensive world of ideas; he must go beyond his little personal aims and adopt the educative purpose of the great fellowship of the liturgy. It goes without saying, therefore, that he is obliged to take part in exercises which do not respond to the particular needs of which he is conscious; that he must ask for things which do not directly concern him; espouse and plead before God causes which do not affect him personally, and which merely arise out of the needs of the community at large; he must at times—and this is inevitable in so richly developed a system of symbols, prayer and action—take part in proceedings of which he does not entirely, if at all, understand the significance.

All this is particularly difficult for modern people, who find it so hard to renounce their independence. And yet people who are perfectly ready to play a subordinate part in state and commercial affairs are all the more susceptible and the more passionately reluctant to regulate their spiritual life by dictates other than those of their private and personal requirements. The requirements of the liturgy can be summed up in one word, humility. Humility by renunciation; that is to say, by the abdication of self-rule and self-sufficiency. And humility by positive action; that is to say, by the acceptance of the spiritual principles which the liturgy offers and which far transcend the little world of individual spiritual existence.

The demands of the liturgy's communal life wear a different aspect for the people who are less affected by its concrete and impersonal side. For the latter, the problem of fellowship does not so much consist in the question of how they are to assimilate the universal and, as it were, concrete element, at the same time subordinating themselves to and dovetailing into it. The difficulty rather lies in their being required to divide their existence with other people, to share the intimacy of their inner life, their feeling and willing, with others; and to know that they are united with these others in a higher unity. And by others we mean not one or two neighbors, or a small circle of people, congenial by reason of similar aims or special relations, but with all, even with those who are indifferent, adverse, or even hostilely-minded.

The demand here resolves itself into the breaking down of the barriers which the more sensitive soul sets around its spiritual life. The soul must issue forth from these if it is to go among others and share their existence. Just as in the first case the community was perceived as a great concrete order, in the second it is perceived as a broad tissue of personal affinities, an endless interweaving of living reciprocal relations. The sacrifice required in the first place is that of renouncing the right of self-determination in spiritual activity; in the second, that of renouncing spiritual isolation. There it is a question of subordinating self to a fixed and objective order, here of sharing life in common with other people. There humility is required, here charity and vigorous expansion of self. There the given spiritual content of the liturgy must be assimilated; here life must be lived in common with the other members of Christ's Body, their petitions included with one's own, their needs voiced as one's own. There "We" is the expression of selfless objectivity; here it signifies that he who employs it is expanding his inner life in order to include that of others, and to assimilate theirs to his. In the first case, the pride which insists upon independence, and the aggressive intolerance often bred by individual existence, must be overcome, while the entire system of communal aims and ideas must be assimilated; in the second, the repulsion occasioned by the strangeness of corporate life must be mastered, and the shrinking from self-expansion, and that exclusiveness triumphed over, which leads us to desire only the company of such as we have ourselves chosen and to whom we have voluntarily opened out. Here, too, is required continual spiritual abnegation, a continuous projection of self at the desire of others, and a great and wonderful love which is ready to participate in their life and to make that life its own.

Yet the subordination of self is actually facilitated by a peculiarity inherent in liturgical life itself. It forms at once the complement of and contrast to what has already been discussed. Let us call the disposition manifesting itself in the two forms indicated above, the individualistic. Facing it stands the social disposition, which eagerly and consistently craves for fellowship, and lives in terms of "We" just as involuntarily as the former bases itself on the exclusive "I." The social disposition will, when it is spiritually active, automatically seek out congenial associates; and their joint striving towards union will be characterized by a firmness and decision alien to the liturgy. It is sufficient to recall in this connection the systems of spiritual association and fellowship peculiar to certain sects. Here at times the bounds of personality diminish to such an extent that all spiritual reserve is lost, and frequently all external reserve as well. Naturally this description only applies to extreme cases, but it still shows the tendency of the social urge in such dispositions. For this reason people like this will not find all their expectations immediately fulfilled in the liturgy. The fellowship of the liturgy will to them appear frigid and restricted. From which it follows that this fellowship, however complete and genuine it may be, still acts as a check upon unconditional self-surrender. The social urge is opposed by an equally powerful tendency which sees to it that a certain fixed boundary is maintained. The individual is, it is true, a member of the whole—but he is only a member. He is not utterly merged in it; he is added to it, but in such a way that he throughout remains an entity, existing of himself. This is notably borne out by the fact that the union of the members is not directly accomplished from man to man. It is accomplished by and in their joint aim, goal, and spiritual resting place—God— by their identical creed, sacrifice and sacraments. In the liturgy it is of very rare occurrence that speech and response, and action or gesture are immediately directed from one member of the fellowship to the other.[15] When this does occur, it is generally worth while to observe the great restraint which characterizes such communication. It is governed by strict regulations. The individual is never drawn into contacts which are too extensively direct. He is always free to decide how far he is to get into touch, from the spiritual point of view, with others in that which is common to them all, in God. Take the kiss of peace, for instance; when it is performed according to the rubric it is a masterly manifestation of restrained and elevated social solidarity.

---

[15] This does not apply, of course, to the communication between the hierarchical persons and the faithful. This relation is continual and direct.

This is of great importance. It is hardly necessary to point out what would be the infallible consequences of attempting to transmit the consciousness of their fellowship in the liturgy directly from one individual to another. The history of the sects teems with examples bearing on this point. For this reason the liturgy sets strict bounds between individuals. Their union is moderated by a continually watchful sentiment of disparity and by reciprocal reverence. Their fellowship notwithstanding, the one individual can never force his way into the intimacy of the other, never influence the latter's prayers and actions, nor force upon the latter his own characteristics, feelings and perceptions. Their fellowship consists in community of intention, thought and language, in the direction of eyes and heart to the one aim; it consists in their identical belief, the identical sacrifice which they offer, the Divine Food which nourishes them all alike; in the one God and Lord Who unites them mystically in Himself. But individuals in their quality of distinct corporeal entities do not among themselves intrude upon each other's inner life.

It is this reserve alone which in the end makes fellowship in the liturgy possible; but for it the latter would be unendurable. By this reserve again the liturgy keeps all vulgarizing elements at a distance. It never allows the soul to feel that it is imprisoned with others, or that its independence and intimacy are threatened with invasion.

From the man of individualistic disposition, then, a sacrifice for the good of the community is required; from the man of social disposition, submission to the austere restraint which characterizes liturgical fellowship. While the former must accustom himself to frequenting the company of his fellows, and must acknowledge that he is only a man among men, the latter must learn to subscribe to the noble, restrained forms which etiquette requires in the House and at the Court of the Divine Majesty.

THE STYLE OF THE LITURGY

Style is chiefly spoken of in a universal sense. By style we understand those particular characteristics which distinguish every valid and genuine production or organism as such, whether it is a work of art, a personality, a form of society, or anything whatever; it denotes that any given vital principle has found its true and final expression. But this self-expression must be of such a nature that it simultaneously imparts to the individual element a universal significance, reaching far beyond its own particular sphere. For the essence of individuality embraces within itself a second element; it is true that it is particular and unreproducible, but it is at the same time universal, standing in relationship to the other individuals of its kind, and manifesting in its permanent existence traits which are also borne by others. The greater the originality and forcefulness of an individual thing, the greater its capacity of comprehensively revealing the universal essence of its kind,[1] the greater is its significance. Now if a personality, a work of art, or a form of society has, by virtue of its existence and activity, expressed in a convincing manner that which it really is, and if at the same time by its quality of specialness it does not merely represent an arbitrary mood, but its relation to a corporate life, then and to that extent it may be said to have style.

In this sense the liturgy undoubtedly has created a style. It is unnecessary to waste further words on the subject.

---

[1] The essence of genius, of the man of genius (e.g., of the Saint), and of the really great work or deed consists in this, that it is immeasurably original and yet is still universally applicable to human life.

The conception can, however, be given a narrower sense. Why is it that in front of a Greek temple we are more intensely conscious of style than we are in front of a Gothic cathedral? The inner effect of both these structures is identically powerful and convincing. Each is the perfect expression of a particular type or form of space-perception. Each reveals the individuality of a people, but at the same time affords a profound insight into the human soul and the significance of the world in general. Yet before the temple of Paestum we are more strongly conscious of style than we are before the cathedrals of Cologne and of Rheims. What is the reason? Why is it that for the uncultured observer Giotto has the more style in comparison with Grünewald, who is without any doubt equally powerful; and the figure of an Egyptian king more than Donatello's wonderful statue of St. John?

In this connection the word *style* has a specialized meaning. It conveys that in the works of art to which reference has been made the individual yields place to the universal. The fortuitous element—determined by place and time, with its significance restricted to certain specific people—is superseded by that which is essentially, or at least more essentially, intended for many times, places and people. The particular is to a great degree absorbed by the universal and ideal. In such works an involved mental or spiritual condition, for instance, which could only have expressed itself in an abstruse utterance or in an unreproducible action, is simplified and reduced to its elements.[2] By this process it is made universally comprehensible. The incalculable ebullition is given a permanent basis. It then becomes easily penetrable and capable of demonstrating in itself the interweaving of cause and effect.[3] The solitary historical event serves to throw into relief the vital significance, universal and unaffected by time, which reposes within it. The fig-

---

[2] Cf. the inner life in Ibsen's plays, for instance, with that of Sophoclean tragedy, the "Ghosts," perhaps, with "Oedipus."

[3] Cf. the line of action adopted by, e.g., Hedda Gabler and Antigone.

ure which appears but once is made to personify characteristics common to the whole of society. The hasty, impetuous movement is restrained and measured. Whereas it was formerly confined to specific relationships or circumstances, it can now to a certain degree be accepted by everyone.[4] Things, materials and instruments are divested of their fortuitous character, their elements revealed, their purpose defined, and their power of expressing certain moods or ideas is heightened.[5] In a word, while one type of art and of life is endeavoring to express that which is special and particular, this other, on the contrary, is striving to hold up to our view that which is universally significant. The latter type of art fashions simple reality, which is always specialized, in such a manner that the ideal and universal comes to the fore; that is to say, its style is developed and its form is fixed. And so whenever life, with its entanglements and its multiplicity, has been simplified in this way, whenever its inner lawfulness is emphasized and it is raised from the particular to the universal, we are always conscious of style in the narrower sense of the word. Admittedly it is difficult to say where style ends and arrangement begins. If the arrangement is too accentuated, if the modeling is carried out according to rules and ideas, and not according to its vital connection with reality, if the production is the result, not of exact observation, but of deliberate planning, then it will be universal only, and therefore lifeless and void.[6] True style, even in its strictest form, still retains the developed faculty of convincing expression. Only that which is living has style; pure thought, and the productions of pure thought, have none.

Now the liturgy—at any rate, as far as the greater part of its range is concerned—has style in the stricter sense of the word. It is not the direct expression of any particular type of spiritual disposi-

---

[4] Such is the origin of social deportment and of court usage.
[5] Such is the origin of symbols—social, state, religious and otherwise.
[6] It is this which differentiates various classical periods from the classical age.

tion, either in its language and ideas, or in its movements, actions and the materials which it employs. If we compare, for instance, the Sunday Collects with the prayers of an Anselm of Canterbury, or of a Newman; the gestures of the officiating priest with the involuntary movements of the man who fancies himself unobserved while at prayer; the Church's directions on the adornment of the sanctuary, on vestments and altar-vessels, with popular methods of decoration, and of dress on religious occasions; and Gregorian chant with the popular hymn—we shall always find, within the sphere of the liturgy, that the medium of spiritual expression, whether it consists of words, gestures, colors or materials, is to a certain degree divested of its singleness of purpose, intensified, tranquilized, and given universal currency.

Many causes have contributed to this result. For one thing, the passing centuries have continually polished, elaborated and adapted the form of liturgical expression Then the strongly generalizing effect of religious thought must be taken into account. Finally, there is the influence of the Greco-Latin spirit, with its highly significant tendency towards style in the strict sense of the word.

Now if we consider the fact that these quietly constructive forces were at work on the vital form of expression, not of an individual, but of an organic unity, composed of the greatness, exclusiveness and strength of the collective consciousness that is the Catholic Church; if we consider further that the vital formula thus fashioned steadily concentrates its whole attention upon the hereafter, that it aspires from this world to the next, and as a natural result is characterized by eternal, sublime and superhuman traits, then we shall find assembled here all the preliminary conditions essential to the development of a style of great vigor and intensity. If it were capable of doing so anywhere, here above all should develop a living style, spiritual, lofty and exalted. And that is precisely what has happened. If we reflect upon the liturgy as a whole, and upon its important points, not upon the abbreviated form in which it is

usually presented, but as it should be, we shall have the good for-
tune to experience the miracle of a truly mighty style. We shall see
and feel that an inner world of immeasurable breadth and depth
has created for itself so rich and so ample an expression and one at
the same time so lucid and so universal in form that its like has
never been seen, either before or since.

And it is style in the stricter sense of the word as well—clear
in language, measured in movement, severe in its modeling of space,
materials, colors and sounds; its ideas, languages, ceremonies and
imagery fashioned out of the simple elements of spiritual life; rich,
varied and lucid; its force further intensified by the fact that the
liturgy employs a classic language, remote from everyday life.

When all these considerations are borne in mind it is easy to
understand that the liturgy possesses a tremendously compelling
form of expression, which is a school of religious training and development to the Catholic who rightly understands it, and which is
bound to appear to the impartial observer as a cultural formation of
the most lofty and elevated kind.

It cannot, however, be denied that great difficulties lie in the
question of the adaptability of the liturgy to every individual, and
more especially to the modern man. The latter wants to find in
prayer—particularly if he is of an independent turn of mind—the
direct expression of his spiritual condition. Yet in the liturgy he is
expected to accept, as the mouthpiece of his inner life, a system of
ideas, prayer and action, which is too highly generalized, and, as it
were, unsuited to him. It strikes him as being formal and almost
meaningless. He is especially sensible of this when he compares
the liturgy with the natural outpourings of spontaneous prayer. Liturgical formulas, unlike the language of a person who is spiritually congenial, are not to be grasped straightway without any further mental exertion on the listener's part; liturgical actions have
not the same direct appeal as, say, the involuntary movement of
understanding on the part of someone who is sympathetic by rea-

son of circumstances and disposition; the emotional impulses of the liturgy do not so readily find an echo as does the spontaneous utterance of the soul. These clear-cut formulas are liable to grate more particularly upon the modern man, so intensely sensitive in everything which affects his scheme of life, who looks for a touch of nature everywhere and listens so attentively for the personal note. He easily tends to consider the idiom of the liturgy as artificial, and its ritual as purely formal. Consequently he will often take refuge in forms of prayer and devotional practices whose spiritual value is far inferior to that of the liturgy, but which seem to have one advantage over the latter—that of contemporary, or, at any rate, of congenial origin.

Those who honestly want to come to grips with this problem in all its bearings should for their own guidance note the way in which the figure of Christ is represented, first in the liturgy, and then in the Gospels. In the latter everything is alive; the reader breathes the air of earth; he sees Jesus of Nazareth walking about the streets and among the people, hears His incomparable and persuasive words, and is aware of the heart-to-heart intercourse between Jesus and His followers. The charm of vivid actuality pervades the historical portrait of Christ. He is so entirely one of us, a real person—Jesus, "the Carpenter's Son"—Who lived in Nazareth in a certain street, wore certain clothes, and spoke in a certain manner. That is just what the modern man longs for; and he is made happy by the fact that in this actual historical figure is incarnate the living and eternal Godhead, One with the body, so that He is in the fullest sense of the word "true God and true Man."

But how differently does the figure of Jesus appear in the liturgy! There He is the Sovereign Mediator between God and man, the eternal High-Priest, the divine Teacher, the Judge of the living and of the dead; in His Body, hidden in the Eucharist, He mystically unites all the faithful in the great society that is the Church; He is the God-Man, the Word that was made Flesh. The human element, or—involuntarily the theological expression rises to the lips—the Human Nature certainly remains intact, for the battle against Eutyches was not fought in vain; He is truly and wholly human, with a body and soul which have actually lived. But they are now utterly transformed by the Godhead, rapt into the light of eternity, and remote from time and space. He is the Lord, "sitting at the right hand of the Father," the mystic Christ living on in His Church.

It will be objected that in the Gospels of the Mass we can still follow the historical life of Jesus in its entirety. That is absolutely true. But if we endeavor to listen more attentively, we shall still find that a particular light is thrown on these narratives by their context. They are a part of the Mass, of the *mysterium magnum*, pervaded by the mystery of sacrifice, an integral part of the structure of the particular Sunday office, current season, or ecclesiastical year, swept along by that powerful straining upwards to the Hereafter which runs through the entire liturgy. In this way the contents of the Gospels, which we hear chanted, and in a foreign language, are in their turn woven into the pattern. Of ourselves we come to consider, not the particular traits which they contain, but their eternal, super-historical meaning.

Yet by this the liturgy has not—as Protestantism has sometimes accused it of doing—disfigured the Christ of the Gospels. It has not set forth a frigid intellectual conception instead of the living Jesus.

The Gospels themselves, according to the aims and purpose of the respective Evangelists, stress first one, then another aspect of the personality and activity of Christ. Facing the portrait contained in the first three Gospels, in the Epistles of St. Paul Christ appears as God, mystically living on in His Church and in the souls of those who believe in Him. The Gospel of St. John shows the Word made Flesh, and finally, in the Apocalypse God is made manifest in His eternal splendor. But this does not mean that the historical facts of Christ's human existence are in any way kept back; on the contrary, they are always taken for granted and often purposely emphasized.[7] The liturgy therefore has done nothing that Holy Scripture itself does not do. Without discarding one stroke or trait of the historical figure of Christ, it has, for its own appointed purpose, more strongly stressed the eternal and supertemporal elements of that figure, and for this reason—the liturgy is no mere commemoration of what once existed, but is living and real; it is the enduring life of Jesus Christ in us, and that of the believer in Christ, eternally God and Man.

It is precisely because of this, however, that the difficulty still persists. It is good to make it absolutely clear, since the modern man experiences it more especially. More than one—according to his instinctive impulse—would be content to forego the profoundest knowledge of theology, if as against that it were permitted to him to watch Jesus walking about the streets or to hear the tone in which He addresses a disciple. More than one would be willing to sacrifice the most beautiful liturgical prayer, if in exchange he might meet Christ face to face and speak to Him from the bottom of his heart.

Where is the angle to be found from which this difficulty is to be tackled and overcome? It is in the view that it is hardly permissible to play off the spiritual life of the individual, with its purely personal bearing, against the spiritual life of the liturgy, with its generalizing bias. They are not mutually contradictory; they should both combine in active cooperation.

When we pray on our own behalf only we approach God from an entirely personal standpoint, precisely as we feel inclined or impelled to do according to our feelings and circumstances. That is our right, and the Church would be the last to wish to deprive us of it. Here we live our own life, and are as it were face to face with

[7] As, for instance, in the beginning of the Gospel of St. John.

God.[8] His Face is turned towards us, as to no one else; He belongs to each one of us. It is this power of being a personal God, ever fresh to each of us, equally patient and attentive to each one's wants, which constitutes the inexhaustible wealth of God. The language which we speak on these occasions suits us entirely, and much of it apparently is suited to us alone. We can use it with confidence because God understands it, and there is no one else who needs to do so.

We are, however, not only individuals, but members of a community as well; we are not merely transitory, but something of us belongs to eternity, and the liturgy takes these elements in us into account. In the liturgy we pray as members of the Church; by it we rise to the sphere which transcends the individual order and is therefore accessible to people of every condition, time, and place. For this order of things the style of the liturgy—vital, clear, and universally comprehensible—is the only possible one. The reason for this is that any other type of prayer, based upon one particular set of hypotheses or requirements, would undoubtedly prove a totally unsuitable form for a content of different origin. Only a system of life and thought which is truly Catholic—that is to say, actual and universal—is capable of being universally adopted, without violence to the individual. Yet there is still an element of sacrifice involved in such adoption. Each one is bound to strive within himself, and to rise superior to self. Yet in so doing he is not swallowed up by, and lost in, the majority; on the contrary, he becomes more independent, rich, and versatile.

Both methods of prayer must cooperate. They stand together in a vital and reciprocal relationship. The one derives its light and fruitfulness from the other. In the liturgy the soul learns to move about the wider and more spacious spiritual world. It assimilates—

---

[8] Even if here, as in the whole range of spiritual things, the Church is our guide. But she is so in a different manner than where the liturgy is concerned.

if the comparison is permissible—that freedom and dignified restraint which in human intercourse is acquired by the man who frequents good society, and who limits his self-indulgence by the discipline of time-honored social usage; the soul expands and develops in that width of feeling and clearness of form which together constitute the liturgy, just as it does through familiarity and communion with great works of art. In a word, the soul acquires, in the liturgy, the "grand manner" of the spiritual life—and that is a thing that cannot be too highly prized. On the other hand, as the Church herself reminds us—and the example of the Orders who live by the liturgy is a proof of this—side by side with the liturgy there must continue to exist that private devotion which provides for the personal requirements of the individual, and to which the soul surrenders itself according to its particular circumstances. From the latter liturgical prayer in its turn derives warmth and local color.

If private devotion were nonexistent, and if the liturgy were the final and exclusive form of spiritual exercise, that exercise might easily degenerate into a frigid formula; but if the liturgy were nonexistent—well, our daily observations amply show what would be the consequences, and how fatally they would take effect.

The Symbolism of the Liturgy

In the liturgy the faithful are confronted by a new world, rich in types and symbols, which are expressed in terms of ritual, actions, vestments, implements, places, and hours, all of which are highly significant. Out of this the question arises—what is the precise significance of all this as regards the soul's intercourse with God? God is above space; what has He to do with directions as to specific localities? God is above time; what does time, beginning with the liturgical hours and ending with the ecclesiastical year, matter to Him? God is Simplicity; then how is He concerned with specific ritual, actions and instruments? Let us desist from the attempt to enter more fully into the question, and content ourselves with asking: God is a Spirit—can matter therefore have any significance in the soul's intercourse with Him? Is not the intervention of material things bound to pervert and to degrade this intercourse? And even if we admit that man consists of soul and body, that he is not pure spirit, and therefore as a logical conclusion that a material element will always play a certain part in his spiritual life—must we not regard this as a defect against which we must strive? Should it not be the task of all true religion to come to be the "worship of God in spirit and in truth," and at least to aim at, if not to succeed in, eliminating the bodily and material element as far as possible?

This question penetrates deeply into the essence and nature of the liturgy.

What meaning has matter—regarded as the medium of spiritual receptivity and utterance, of spiritual impression and expression—for us?

The question depends upon the manner in which the Ego, within its bodily-spiritual personality, experiences the relationship between body and soul.[1] There exists a peculiar form of this self-experience, in which the boundary between the "spiritual" and the "bodily" or "physical" is sharply defined. In such cases the spiritual plane appears as entirely self-contained, lying within—or perhaps it would be better to say beyond—the physical plane, and having little or nothing to do with the latter. The two planes—spiritual and physical—are felt to be two distinct orders, lying closely adjacent, between which communication certainly takes place; but communication of such a nature that it rather appears as a transposition from the one into the other, than as the direct cooperation of both. Such is the frame of mind which has probably drawn its conception of the external world from Leibniz's theory of monads, and its conception of the soul from the teaching of psychophysical parallelism.

It is obvious that people who favor such a system of thought will only attach a more or less fortuitous significance to the relationship between the physical and the spiritual. The latter, they consider, is intimately bound up with the former, and is also in need of it, but as far as the life of the soul proper is concerned, the physical has no importance; it merely appears to encumber and to degrade spiritual activity. The soul strives to attain its goal—that is to say, truth, the moral impulse, God, and the Divine—by purely spiritual means. Even when such people know that this endeavor cannot possibly succeed, they still exert themselves to approach to the purely spiritual at least as nearly as they can. To them the physical is an alloy, an innate imperfection, of which they endeavor to rid themselves. They may perhaps credit it with a limited external significance, and look upon it as an aid to the elucidation of the spiritual, as an illustration, or as an allegory; but they are all the

---

[1] The more precise discussion of the question belongs to the domain, as yet but little explored, of typological psychology.

time conscious that they are making what is actually an inadmissible concession. Moreover, the physical does not appeal to them as a medium of vividly expressing their inner life. They scarcely even feel the need of expressing that life in a tangible manner; for them the spiritual is self-sufficing, or else it can express itself in a straightforward moral action and in a simply uttered word.

People of such a turn of mind will inevitably have great difficulties to face in the liturgy.[2] Somewhat naturally, they gravitate towards a strictly spiritual form of devotion, which aims at suppressing the physical or material element and at shaping its external manifestations in as plain and homely a manner as possible; it prizes the simple word as the most spiritual medium of communication.

Facing these, and in contrast with them, are people of a different mental constitution. For them, the spiritual and the physical are inextricably jumbled together;[3] they incline to amalgamate the two. While the former type of disposition labors to separate the physical and the spiritual spheres, the latter endeavors to unite them. People like this are prone to look upon the soul merely as the lining of the body, and upon the body as the outside, in some sort the condensation or materialization, of the spirit within. They interpret spiritual elements in terms of physical conditions or movements, and directly perceive every material action as a spiritual experience. They extend their conviction of the essential oneness of the soul and the body beyond the province of the individual personality, and include external things within its sphere of opera-

---

[2] This disposition does not, of course, actually exist in the extreme form portrayed here any more than does that which is described later. We are concerned, however, with giving an account of such conditions in the abstract and not in detail.

[3] It need hardly be said that no intention exists of discussing in this connection the real relationship of soul and body. We are concerned with describing the manner in which this relationship is felt and interiorly experienced. It is not a question of metaphysics, but merely of descriptive psychology.

tion. As they frequently tend to regard externals as the manifestation of spiritual elements, they are also capable of utilizing them as
a means of expressing their own innerness. They see this expressed
in various substances, in clothing, in social formations, and in Nature, while their inner struggles are reflected even in conditions,
desires, and conflicts which are universal.[4]

Of the two types of spiritual character, the second at the first
glance would seem to correspond the more closely to the nature of
the liturgy. It is far more susceptible to the power of expression
proper to liturgical action and materials, and can the more readily
apply these external phenomena to the expression of its own inner
life. Yet in the liturgy it has to face problems and difficulties all its
own.

People who perceive the physical or material and the spiritual
as inextricably mingled find it hard to confine the manifestations
of the individual soul to set forms of expression, and to adhere
strictly to the clearly defined significance of the formulas, actions
and instruments employed in such expression. They conceive the
inner life as being in a perpetual state of flux. They cannot create
definite and clearly outlined forms of expression because they are
incapable of separating spiritual from physical or material objects.
They find it equally difficult to distinguish clearly the specific substance behind the given forms of expression; they will always give
it a fresh interpretation according to varying circumstances.[5]

In other words, in spite of the close relationship which in this
case exists between the physical and the spiritual, such people lack
the power of welding certain spiritual contents to certain external
forms, which together will constitute either the expression of their
inner selves or a receptacle for an extraneous content. That is to

---

[4] Cf., for instance, the feeling of the Romantics for Nature.

[5] Hence the tendency of people like this to forsake the Church, with her clear
and unequivocal formulas, and to turn to Nature, there to seek an outlet for their
vague and fluctuating emotions, and to win from her the stimulus that suits them.

say, they lack one of the ingredients essential to the creation of symbols. The other type of people do not succeed any better, because they fail to realize how vital the relationship is between the spiritual and the physical. They are perfectly capable of differentiating and of delimiting the boundaries between the two, but they do this to such an extent that they lose all sense of cohesion. The second type possess a sense of cohesion, and with them the inner content issues directly into the external form. But they lack discrimination and objectiveness. Both—the sense of cohesion and the power of discrimination—are essential to the creation of a symbol.

A symbol may be said to originate when that which is interior and spiritual finds expression in that which is exterior and material. But it does not originate when[6] a spiritual element is by general consent coupled with a material substance, as, for instance, the image of the scales with the idea of Justice. Rather must the spiritual element transpose itself into material terms because it is vital and essential that it should do so. Thus the body is the natural emblem of the soul, and a spontaneous physical movement will typify a spiritual event. The symbol proper is circumscribed; and it may be further distinguished by the total inability of the form selected as a medium of expression to represent anything else whatever. It must be expressed in clear and precise terms and therefore, when it has fulfilled the usual conditions, must be universally comprehensible. A genuine symbol is occasioned by the spontaneous expression of an actual and particular spiritual condition. But at the same time, like works of art, it must rise above the purely individual plane. It must not merely express isolated spiritual elements, but deal with life and the soul in the abstract.

Consequently when a symbol has been created, it often enjoys widespread currency and becomes universally comprehensible and

[6] As in allegory.

significant. The auspicious collaboration of both the types of temperament outlined above is essential to the creation of a symbol, in which the spiritual and the physical elements must be united in perfect harmony. At the same time it is the task of the spiritual element to watch over and determine every stroke of the modeling, to sort and sift with a sure hand, to measure off and weigh together delicately and discreetly, in order that the given matter may be given its corresponding and appropriate form. The more clearly and completely a spiritual content is cast in its material mold, the more valuable is the symbol thus produced, and the more worthy it is of its name, because it then loses its connection with the solitary incident which occasioned it and becomes a universal possession. The greater the depth of life from which it has sprung, and the greater the degree of clarity and of conviction which has contributed to its formation, the more true this is in proportion.

The power of symbol-building was at work, for instance, when the fundamental rules governing social intercourse were laid down. From it are derived those forms by which one person signifies to another interest or reverence, in which are externally expressed the inward happenings of civil and political life, and the like. Further—and in this connection it is specially significant—it is the origin of those gestures which convey a spiritual meaning; the man who is moved by emotion will kneel, bow, clasp his hands or impose them, stretch forth his arms, strike his breast, make an offering of something, and so on. These elementary gestures are capable of richer development and expansion, or else of amalgamation. They are the source of the manifold ritual actions, such as the kiss of peace or the blessing. Or it may be that certain ideas are expressed in corresponding movements, thus belief in the mystery of absolution is shown by the Sign of the Cross. Finally, a whole series of such movements may be coordinated. This gives rise to religious action by which a richly developed spiritual element— e.g., a sacrifice—succeeds in attaining external and symbolic expression. It is when that form of self-experience which has been described above is extended to objects which lie without the personal province, that the material concrete factor enters into the symbol. Material objects are used to reinforce the expressiveness of the body and its movements, and at the same time form an extension of the permanent bodily powers. Thus, for instance, in a sacrifice the victim is offered, not only by the hands, but in a vessel or dish. The smooth surface of the dish emphasizes the expressive motion of the hand; it forms a wide and open plane, displayed before the Godhead, and throwing into powerful relief the upward straining line of the arm. Or again, as it rises, the smoke of the incense enhances the aspiration expressed by the upturned hands and gaze of those who are at prayer. The candle, with its slender, soaring, tapering column tipped with flame, and consuming itself as it burns, typifies the idea of sacrifice, which is voluntarily offered in lofty spiritual serenity.

Both the before-mentioned types of temperament cooperate in the creation of symbols. The one, with its apprehension of the affinity between the spiritual and the physical, provides the material for the primary hypothesis essential to the creation of the symbol. The other, by its power of distinction and its objectiveness, brings to the symbol lucidity and form. They both, however, find in the liturgy the problems peculiar to their temperament. But because they have shared together in the creation of the liturgical symbol, both are capable of overcoming these difficulties as soon, that is, as they are at least in some way convinced of the binding value of the liturgy.

The former type, then, must abandon their exaggerated spirituality, admit the existence of the relationship between the spiritual and the physical, and freely avail themselves of the wealth of liturgical symbolism. They must give up their reserve and the Puritanism which prompts them to oppose the expression of the spiritual in material terms, and must instead take the latter as a medium of lively expression. This will add a new warmth and depth to their emotional and spiritual experience.

The latter type must endeavor to stem their extravagance of sensation, and to bind the vague and ephemeral elements into clear-cut forms. It is of the highest importance that they should realize that the liturgy is entirely free from any subjection to matter,[7] and that all the natural elements in the liturgy (cf. what has been previously said concerning its style) are entirely recast as ritual forms. So for people of this type the symbolizing power of the liturgy becomes a school of measure and of spiritual restraint.

The people who really live by the liturgy will come to learn that the bodily movements, the actions, and the material objects which it employs are all of the highest significance. It offers great opportunities of expression, of knowledge, and of spiritual experience; it is emancipating in its action, and capable of presenting a truth far more strongly and convincingly than can the mere word of mouth.

[7] Such as is found in Nature-religions, for instance, which are directly derived from Nature herself, from the forest, the sea, etc. The liturgy, on the contrary, is entirely designed by human hands. It would be extremely interesting to investigate in a detailed manner the transformation of natural things, shapes and sounds into ritual objects through the agency of the liturgy.

THE PLAYFULNESS OF THE LITURGY

Grave and earnest people, who make the knowledge of truth their whole aim, see moral problems in everything, and seek for a definite purpose everywhere, tend to experience a peculiar difficulty where the liturgy is concerned.[1] They incline to regard it as being to a certain extent aimless, as superfluous pageantry of a needlessly complicated and artificial character. They are affronted by the scrupulously exact instructions which the liturgy gives on correct procedure, on the right direction in which to turn, on the pitch of the voice, and so on. What is the use of it all? The essential part of Holy Mass—the action of Sacrifice and the divine Banquet—could be so easily consummated. Why, then, the need for the solemn institution of the priestly office? The necessary consecration could be so simply accomplished in so few words, and the sacraments so straightforwardly administered—what is the reason of all the prayers and ceremonies? The liturgy tends to strike people of this turn of mind as—to use the words which are really most appropriate—trifling and theatrical.

The question is a serious one. It does not occur to everyone, but in the people whom it does affect it is a sign of the mental attitude which concentrates on and pursues that which is essential. It appears to be principally connected with the question of purpose.

---

[1] In what follows the writer must beg the reader not to weigh isolated words and phrases. The matter under consideration is vague and intangible, and not easy to put into words. The writer can only be sure of not being misunderstood if the reader considers the chapter and the general train of thought as a whole.

That which we call purpose is, in the true sense of the word, the distributive, organizing principle which subordinates actions or objects to other actions or objects, so that the one is directed towards the other, and one exists for the sake of the other. That which is subordinate, the means, is only significant in so far as it is capable of serving that which is superior, the end. The purpose does not infuse a spiritual value into its medium; it uses it as a passage to something else, a thoroughfare merely; aim and fulcrum alike reside in the former. From this point of view, every instrument has to prove in the first place whether, and in the second to what extent, it is fitted to accomplish the purpose for which it is employed. This proof will primarily be headed by the endeavor to eliminate from the instrument all the nonessential, unimportant, and superfluous elements. It is a scientific principle that an end should be attained with the minimum expenditure of energy, time, and material. A certain restless energy, an indifference to the cost involved, and accuracy in going to the point, characterize the corresponding turn of mind.

A disposition like this is, on the whole, both appropriate and necessary to life, giving it earnestness and fixity of purpose. It also takes reality into consideration, to the extent of viewing everything from the standpoint of purpose. Many pursuits and professions can be shown to have their origin almost entirely in the idea of purpose. Yet no phenomenon can be entirely, and many can be, to a minor degree only, comprehended in this category. Or, to put it more plainly, that which gives objects and events their right to existence, and justifies their individuality, is in many cases not the sole, and in others not even the primary reason for their usefulness. Are flowers and leaves useful? Of course; they are the vital organs of plants. Yet because of this, they are not tied down to any particular form, color, or smell. Then what, upon the whole, is the use of the extravagance of shapes, colors and scents, in Nature? To what purpose the multiplicity of species? Things could be so much more simple. Nature could be entirely filled with animate beings, and they could thrive and progress in a far quicker and more suitable manner. The indiscriminate application to Nature of the idea of purpose is, however, open to objection. To go to the root of the matter, what is the object of this or that plant, and of this or that animal, existing at all? Is it in order to afford nourishment to some other plant or animal? Of course not. Measured merely by the standard of apparent and external utility, there is a great deal in Nature which is only partially, and nothing which is wholly and entirely, intended for a purpose, or, better still, purpose*ful*. Indeed, considered in this light, a great deal is purposeless. In a mechanical structure—a machine, say, or a bridge—everything has a purpose; and the same thing applies to business enterprises or to the government of a State; yet even where these phenomena are concerned, the idea of purpose is not far-reaching enough to give an adequate reply to the query, whence springs their right to existence?

If we want to do justice to the whole question, we must shift our angle of vision. The conception of purpose regards an object's center of gravity as existing outside that object, seeing it lie instead in the transition to further movement, i.e., that towards the goal which the object provides. But every object is to a certain extent, and many are entirely, self-sufficient and an end in itself—if, that is, the conception can be applied at all in this extensive sense. The conception of meaning is more adaptable. Objects which have no purpose in the strict sense of the term have a meaning. This meaning is not realized by their extraneous effect or by the contribution which they make to the stability or the modification of another object, but their significance consists in being what they are. Measured by the strict sense of the word, they are purposeless, but still full of meaning.

Purpose and meaning are the two aspects of the fact that an existent principle possesses the motive for, and the right to, its own essence and existence. An object regarded from the point of view

of purpose is seen to dovetail into an order of things which comprehends both it and more beyond it; from the standpoint of meaning, it is seen to be based upon itself.

Now what is the meaning of that which exists? That it should
exist and should be the image of God the Everlasting. And what is
the meaning of that which is alive? That it should live, bring forth
its essence, and bloom as a natural manifestation of the living God.

This is true of Nature. It is also true of the life of the soul. Has
science an aim or an object in the real sense of the word? No. Pragmatism is trying to foist one upon it. It insists that the aim of science is to better humanity and to improve it from the moral point
of view. Yet this constitutes a failure to appreciate the independent
value of knowledge. Knowledge has no aim, but it has a meaning,
and one that is rooted in itself—truth. The legislative activity of
Parliament, for instance, has an end in view; it is intended to bring
about a certain agreed result in the life of the State. Jurisprudence,
on the contrary, has no object; it merely indicates where truth lies
in questions of law. The same thing applies to all real science. According to its nature, it is either the knowledge of truth or the service of truth, but nothing else. Has art any aim or purpose? No, it
has not. If it had, we should be obliged to conclude that art exists in
order to provide a living for artists, or else, as the eighteenth century German thinkers of the *Aufklärung*—the "age of enlightenment"—considered, it is intended to offer concrete examples of
intelligent views and to inculcate virtue. This is absolutely untrue.
The work of art has no purpose, but it has a meaning—"*ut sit*"—
that it should exist, and that it should clothe in clear and genuine
form the essence of things and the inner life of the human artist. It
is merely to be "*splendor veritatis*," the glory of truth.

When life lacks the austere guidance of the sense of purpose it
degenerates into pseudo-aestheticism. But when it is forced into
the rigid framework that is the purely purposeful conception of the
world, it droops and perishes. The two conceptions are interdepen-

dent. Purpose is the goal of all effort, labor and organization; meaning is the essence of existence, of flourishing, ripening life. Purpose and meaning, effort and growth, activity and production, organization and creation—these are the two poles of existence.

The life of the Universal Church is also organized on these lines. In the first place, there is the whole tremendous system of purposes incorporated in the Canon Law, and in the constitution and government of the Church. Here we find every means directed to the one end, that of keeping in motion the great machinery of ecclesiastical government. The first-mentioned point of view will decide whether adjustment or modification best serves the collective purpose, and whether the latter is attained with the least possible expenditure of time and energy.[2] The scheme of labor must be arranged and controlled by a strictly practical spirit.

The Church, however, has another side. It embraces a sphere which is in a special sense free from purpose. And that is the liturgy. The latter certainly comprehends a whole system of aims and purposes, as well as the instruments to accomplish them. It is the business of the Sacraments to act as the channels of certain graces. This mediation, however, is easily and quickly accomplished when the necessary conditions are present. The administration of the Sacraments is an example of a liturgical action which is strictly confined to the one object. Of course, it can be said of the liturgy, as of every action and every prayer which it contains, that it is directed towards the providing of spiritual instruction. This is perfectly true. But the liturgy has no thought-out, deliberate, detailed plan of instruction. In order to sense the difference it is sufficient to compare a week of the ecclesiastical year with the Spiritual Exercises of St. Ignatius. In the latter every element is determined by deliberate choice, everything is directed towards the production of a certain

---

[2] Even when the Church is considered from its other aspect, that of a Divine work of art. Yet the former conception is bound to recur in this connection.

spiritual and didactic result; each exercise, each prayer, even the way in which the hours of repose are passed, all aim at the one thing, the conversion of the will. It is not so with the liturgy. The fact that the latter has no place in the Spiritual Exercises is a proof of this.[3] The liturgy wishes to teach, but not by means of an artificial system of aim-conscious educational influences; it simply creates an entire spiritual world in which the soul can live according to the requirements of its nature. The difference resembles that which exists between a gymnasium, in which every detail of the apparatus and every exercise aims at a calculated effect, and the open woods and fields. In the first everything is consciously directed towards discipline and development, in the second life is lived with Nature, and internal growth takes place in her. The liturgy creates a universe brimming with fruitful spiritual life, and allows the soul to wander about in it at will and to develop itself there. The abundance of prayers, ideas, and actions, and the whole arrangement of the calendar are incomprehensible when they are measured by the objective standard of strict suitability for a purpose. The liturgy has no purpose, or, at least, it cannot be considered from the standpoint of purpose. It is not a means which is adapted to attain a certain end—it is an end in itself. This fact is important, because if we overlook it, we labor to find all kinds of didactic purposes in the liturgy which may certainly be stowed away somewhere, but are not actually evident.

When the liturgy is rightly regarded, it cannot be said to have a purpose, because it does not exist for the sake of humanity, but for the sake of God. In the liturgy man is no longer concerned with himself; his gaze is directed towards God. In it man is not so much intended to edify himself as to contemplate God's majesty. The liturgy means that the soul exists in God's presence, originates in

---

[3] The Benedictines give it one, but do so in an obviously different system of spiritual exercises to that conceived by St. Ignatius.

Him, lives in a world of divine realities, truths, mysteries and symbols, and really lives its true, characteristic and fruitful life.[4]

There are two very profound passages in Holy Scripture, which are quite decisive on the point. One is found in the description of Ezekiel's vision.[5] Let us consider the flaming Cherubim, who "every one of them went straight forward, whither the impulse of the Spirit was to go . . . , and they turned not when they went . . . , ran and returned like flashes of lightning . . . , went . . . and stood . . . and were lifted up from the earth . . . , the noise of their wings was like the noise of many waters . . . , and when they stood, their wings were let down." How "aimless" they are! How discouraging for the zealous partisans of reasonable suitability for a purpose! They are only pure motion, powerful and splendid, acting according to the direction of the Spirit, desiring nothing save to express Its inner drift and Its interior glow and force. They are the living image of the liturgy.

In the second passage it is Eternal Wisdom which speaks: "I was with Him, forming all things, and was delighted every day, playing before Him at all times, playing in the world. . . ."[6]

This is conclusive. It is the delight of the Eternal Father that Wisdom (the Son, the perfect Fullness of Truth) should pour out Its eternal essence before Him in all Its ineffable splendor, without any "purpose"—for what purpose should It have?—but full of decisive meaning, in pure and vocal happiness; the Son "plays" before the Father.

Such is the life of the highest beings, the angels, who, without a purpose and as the Spirit stirs them, move before God, and are a mystic diversion and a living song before Him.

---

[4] The fact that the liturgy moralizes so little is consistent with this conception. In the liturgy the soul forms itself, not by means of deliberate teaching and the exercise of virtue, but by the fact that it exists in the light of eternal Truth, and is naturally and supernaturally robust.

[5] Ezekiel 1. 4 et seq., especially 12, 17, 20, 24, and x. 9 et seq.

[6] Proverbs viii 30, 31.

In the earthly sphere there are two phenomena which tend in the same direction: the play of the child and the creation of the artist.

The child, when it plays, does not aim at anything. It has no purpose. It does not want to do anything but to exercise its youthful powers, pour forth its life in an aimless series of movements, words and actions, and by this to develop and to realize itself more fully; all of which is purposeless, but full of meaning nevertheless, the significance lying in the unchecked revelation of this youthful life in thoughts and words and movements and actions, in the capture and expression of its nature, and in the fact of its existence. And because it does not aim at anything in particular, because it streams unbroken and spontaneously forth, its utterance will be harmonious, its form clear and fine; its expression will of itself become picture and dance, rhyme, melody and song. That is what play means; it is life, pouring itself forth without an aim, seizing upon riches from its own abundant store, significant through the fact of its existence. It will be beautiful, too, if it is left to itself, and if no futile advice and pedagogic attempts at enlightenment foist upon it a host of aims and purposes, thus denaturizing it.

Yet, as life progresses, conflicts ensue, and it appears to grow ugly and discordant. Man sets before himself what he wants to do and what he should do, and tries to realize this in his life. But in the course of these endeavors he learns that many obstacles stand in his way, and he perceives that it is very seldom that he can attain his ideal.

It is in a different order, in the imaginary sphere of representation, that man tries to reconcile the contradiction between that which he wishes to be and that which he is. In art he tries to harmonize the ideal and actuality, that which he ought to be and that which he is, the soul within and nature without, the body and the soul. Such are the visions of art. It has no didactic aims, then; it is not intended to inculcate certain truths and virtues. A true artist has never had such an end in view. In art, he desires to do nothing but to overcome the discord to which we have referred, and to express in the sphere of representation the higher life of which he stands in need, and to which in actuality he has only approximately attained. The artist merely wants to give life to his being and its longings, to give external form to the inner truth. And people who contemplate a work of art should not expect anything of it but that they should be able to linger before it, moving freely, becoming conscious of their own better nature, and sensing the fulfillment of their most intimate longings. But they should not reason and chop logic, or look for instruction and good advice from it.

The liturgy offers something higher. In it man, with the aid of grace, is given the opportunity of realizing his fundamental essence, of really becoming that which according to his divine destiny he should be and longs to be, a child of God. In the liturgy he is to go "unto God, Who giveth joy to his youth."[7] All this is, of course, on the supernatural plane, but at the same time it corresponds to the same degree to the inner needs of man's nature. Because the life of the liturgy is higher than that to which customary reality gives both the opportunity and form of expression, it adopts suitable forms and methods from that sphere in which alone they are to be found, that is to say, from art. It speaks measuredly and melodiously; it employs formal, rhythmic gestures; it is clothed in colors and garments foreign to everyday life; it is carried out in places and at hours which have been coordinated and systematized according to sublimer laws than ours. It is in the highest sense the life of a child, in which everything is picture, melody and song.

Such is the wonderful fact which the liturgy demonstrates; it unites art and reality in a supernatural childhood before God. That which formerly existed in the world of unreality only, and was rendered in art as the expression of mature human life, has here

---

[7] Entrance prayer of the Mass.

become reality. These forms are the vital expression of real and frankly supernatural life. But this has one thing in common with the play of the child and the life of art—it has no purpose, but it is full of profound meaning. It is not work, but play. To be at play, or to fashion a work of art in God's sight—not to create, but to exist—such is the essence of the liturgy. From this is derived its sublime mingling of profound earnestness and divine joyfulness. The fact that the liturgy gives a thousand strict and careful directions on the quality of the language, gestures, colors, garments and instruments which it employs, can only be understood by those who are able to take art and play seriously. Have you ever noticed how gravely children draw up the rules of their games, on the form of the melody, the position of the hands, the meaning of this stick and that tree? It is for the sake of the silly people who may not grasp their meaning and who will persist in seeing the justification of an action or object only in its obvious purpose. Have you ever read of or even experienced the deadly earnestness with which the artist-vassal labors for art, his lord? Of his sufferings on the score of language? Or of what an overweening mistress form is? And all this for something that has no aim or purpose! No, art does not bother about aims. Does anyone honestly believe that the artist would take upon himself the thousand anxieties and feverish perplexities incident to creation if he intended to do nothing with his work but to teach the spectator a lesson, which he could just as well express in a couple of facile phrases, or one or two historical examples, or a few well-taken photographs? The only answer to this can be an emphatic negative. Being an artist means wrestling with the expression of the hidden life of man, avowedly in order that it may be given existence; nothing more. It is the image of the Divine creation, of which it is said that it has made things "*ut sint.*"

The liturgy does the same thing. It too, with endless care, with all the seriousness of the child and the strict conscientiousness of the great artist, has toiled to express in a thousand forms the sacred, God-given life of the soul to no other purpose than that the soul may therein have its existence and live its life. The liturgy has laid down the serious rules of the sacred game which the soul plays before God. And, if we are desirous of touching bottom in this mystery, it is the Spirit of fire and of holy discipline "Who has knowledge of the world"[8] —the Holy Ghost—Who has ordained the game which the Eternal Wisdom plays before the Heavenly Father in the Church, Its kingdom on earth. And "Its delight" is in this way "to be with the children of men."

Only those who are not scandalized by this understand what the liturgy means. From the very first every type of rationalism has turned against it. The practice of the liturgy means that by the help of grace, under the guidance of the Church, we grow into living works of art before God, with no other aim or purpose than that of living and existing in His sight; it means fulfilling God's Word and "becoming as little children"; it means foregoing maturity with all its purposefulness, and confining oneself to play, as David did when he danced before the Ark. It may, of course, happen that those extremely clever people, who merely from being grown-up have lost all spiritual youth and spontaneity, will misunderstand this and jibe at it. David probably had to face the derision of Michal.

It is in this very aspect of the liturgy that its didactic aim is to be found, that of teaching the soul not to see purposes everywhere, not to be too conscious of the end it wishes to attain, not to be desirous of being over clever and grown-up, but to understand simplicity in life. The soul must learn to abandon, at least in prayer, the restlessness of purposeful activity; it must learn to waste time for the sake of God, and to be prepared for the sacred game with sayings and thoughts and gestures, without always immediately asking "why?" and "wherefore?" It must learn not to be continually yearning to do something, to attack something, to accomplish

[8] Responsory at Terce, Pentecost.

something useful, but to play the divinely ordained game of the liturgy in liberty and beauty and holy joy before God.

In the end, eternal life will be its fulfillment. Will the people who do not understand the liturgy be pleased to find that the heavenly consummation is an eternal song of praise? Will they not rather associate themselves with those other industrious people who consider that such an eternity will be both boring and unprofitable?

THE SERIOUSNESS OF THE LITURGY

The liturgy is art, translated into terms of life. Sensitive people clearly recognize its wealth of expression, its symmetry of form, and its delicate sense of proportion. As a result, such people are in danger of appreciating the Church's worship merely for the sake of its aesthetic value. It is on the whole understandable that poetic literature should apprehend the liturgy from its artistic side. It is a more serious matter when this is so emphatically stressed in writings which are particularly dedicated to liturgical worship. It is sufficient for our purpose to recall valuable works such as Staudenmaier's "Geist des Christentums," or many of J. K. Huysman's books, "L'Oblat," for instance. The present writer is anxious that this little work should not gravitate, however unconsciously, in the same direction. For this reason, in the chapter which has been begun, the question will be more closely examined.

It is an incontrovertible proposition that people who consider a work of art merely from the artistic point of view do it an injustice. Its significance as a composition can only be fully estimated when it is viewed in connection with the whole of life. A work of art is in less danger from the logician or the moral philosopher pure and simple, because they stand in no particular relation to it. Deadly destructive to the work of art, however, is the purely artistic perception of the aesthete—both word and matter being taken in the worst and most extreme sense which they have possessed since, for instance, Oscar Wilde.

Still more does this hold good when it is a question, not of the representation of a work of art, but of actual people, and even of that tremendous unity—the *Opus Dei*, that is the liturgy—in which the Creator-Artist, the Holy Ghost, has garnered and expressed the whole fullness of reality and of creative art. Aesthetes are everywhere looked upon as unwelcome guests, as drones and as parasites sponging on life, but nowhere are they more deserving of anger and contempt than in the sphere of sacred things. The careworn man who seeks nothing at Mass but the fulfillment of the service which he owes to his God; the busy woman, who comes to be a little lightened of her burden; the many people who, barren of feeling and perceiving nothing of the beauty and splendor of word and sound which surrounds them, but merely seek strength for their daily toil—all these penetrate far more deeply into the essence of the liturgy than does the connoisseur who is busy savoring the contrast between the austere beauty of a Preface and the melodiousness of a Gradual.

All of which impels us to the fundamental question, what is the importance of beauty in relation to the entire liturgical scheme?

First, however, a slight but necessary digression. We have already seen that the Church's life functions in two directions. On the one side there exists an active communal life, a tremendous driving force of systematically directed activities, which, however, coalesce in the many-membered but strongly centralized organization. Such a unity alike presupposes and manifests power. But what is the purpose of power in the spiritual sphere?

This query deeply concerns every one of us, each according to his disposition. For the one, it is a question of satisfying himself as to the truth of the axiom that every type of society, including the spiritual, needs power if it is to subsist. The truth of this does not degrade the ideal, even if it ranks power next in order to doctrine, exhortation, and organization. This external power must not of course be allowed to usurp the place of truth and of justice, nor permitted to influence convictions. Where, however, a religion is concerned which does not confine itself to presenting ideals and

opinions, but undertakes the molding and adapting of human entities on behalf of the Kingdom of God, there power is necessary. It
is this which adapts a truth, or a spiritual or ethical system, to the
needs of actual existence.

But if there are people who find it hard to bear that things like
justice and power should be named in the same breath with such
intimate matters as religious convictions and spiritual life, there
are others who are entirely differently constituted. Upon such people
a tremendous force like the Catholic Church produces so direct an
effect that they easily forget the real significance of such power. It
is merely a means to an end. It is a tool, used to carve the Kingdom
of God from the raw material of the world; it is the servant of
Divine truth and grace. If an attempt were to be made to constitute
a form of spiritual society without a powerful discipline, it would
inevitably dissolve into fleeting shadows. But if power, the servant, were to be promoted to the position of master, the means to
that of the end, the tool to that of the guiding hand, religion would
then be stifled by despotism and its consequence, slavery.

Somewhat analogous to the position of power in the Church's
active life is that of beauty in relation to her contemplative side.
The Church not only exists for a purpose, but she is of herself
significant, viewed from her other aspect of art transformed into
life—or, better still, in the process of transformation. For that is
what the Church is in the liturgy.

The preceding chapter endeavored to demonstrate that artistic
self-sufficiency is actually compatible with the liturgy. Only a soph-
ist could argue that the justification of a form of life resides exclusively in its manifest purposes. On the other hand, one must not
forget as well that artistic worth—beauty—is as dangerous to the
susceptible person as is power in the corresponding sphere of active communal life. The danger inherent in the idea of power is
only to be overcome by those who are clear about its nature and
the method of employing it. Similarly, only those who force their

way into perception of its import can break free from the illusive spell of beauty.

Apart from this stands the question, whence a spiritual value derives its currency, whether from itself or from an extraneous superior value? Associated with it, but entirely distinct, is the second question, as to the quality of the relation which exists between one value which is admittedly based upon itself and other independent values. The first question endeavors to trace one value back to another, e.g., the validity of the administration of justice to justice in the abstract. The second investigates the existence, between two values of equal validity, of a determinate order which may not be inverted.

Truth is of itself a value, because it is truth, justice because it is justice, and beauty because and in so far as it is beauty. No one of these qualities can derive its validity from another, but only from itself.[1] The most profound and true thought does not make a work beautiful, and the best intentions of the artist avail as little, if his creation, in addition to a concrete, vivid and robust form, has not—in a word—beauty. Beauty as such is valid of itself, entirely independent of truth and other values. An object or a work of art is beautiful, when its inner essence and significance find perfect expression in its existence. This perfection of expression embraces the fact of beauty, and is its accepted form of currency. Beauty means that the essence of an object or action has, from the first moment of its existence and from the innermost depths of its being, formulated its relation to the universe and to the spiritual world; that this interior formation, from which has developed a phenomenon susceptible of expression, has resolved upon symbolic unity; that everything is said which should be said, and no more; that the essential form is attained, and no other; that in it there is nothing

---

[1] We are not concerned here with the question if and how all forms of validity ultimately go back to an ultimately valid Absolute, i.e., to God.

that is lifeless and empty, but everything that is vivid and animated; that every sound, every word, every surface, shade and movement, emanates from within, contributes to the expression of the whole, and is associated with the rest in a seamless, organic unity. Beauty is the full, clear and inevitable expression of the inner truth in the external manifestation. *"Pulchritudo est splendor veritatis"*—"*est species boni*," says ancient philosophy, "beauty is the splendid perfection which dwells in the revelation of essential truth and goodness."

Beauty, therefore, is an independent value; it is not truth and not goodness, nor can it be derived from them. And yet it stands in the closest relation to these other values. As we have already remarked, in order that beauty may be made manifest, something must exist which will reveal itself externally; there must be an essential truth which compels utterance, or an event which will out. Pride of place, therefore, though not of rank or worth, belongs, not to beauty, but to truth. Although this applies incontestably to life as a whole, and to the fundamentals of art as well, it will perhaps be difficult for the artist to accept without demur.

"Beauty is the splendor of truth," says scholastic philosophy. To us moderns this sounds somewhat frigid and superficially dogmatic. But if we remember that this axiom was held and taught by men who were incomparable constructive thinkers, who conceived ideas, framed syllogisms, and established systems, which still tower over others like vast cathedrals, we shall feel it incumbent upon us to penetrate more deeply into the meaning of these few words. Truth does not mean mere lifeless accuracy of comprehension, but the right and appropriate regulation of life, a vital spiritual essence; it means the intrinsic value of existence in all its force and fullness. And beauty is the triumphant splendor which breaks forth when the hidden truth is revealed, when the external phenomenon is at all points the perfect expression of the inner essence. Perfection of expression, then, not merely superficial and external, but interior and contemporaneous with every step in the creation—can the essence of beauty be more profoundly and at the same time more briefly defined?

Beauty cannot be appreciated unless this fact is borne in mind, and it is apprehended as the splendor of perfectly expressed intrinsic truth.

But there is a grave risk, which many people do not escape, of this order being reversed, and of beauty being placed before truth, or treated as entirely separate from the latter, the perfection of form from the content, and the expression from its substance and meaning. Such is the danger incurred by the aesthetic conception of the world, which ultimately degenerates into nerveless aestheticism.

No investigation of the aesthetic mind and ideas can be undertaken here. But we may premise that its primary characteristic is a more or less swift withdrawal from discussion of the reason for a thing's existence to the manner of it, from the content to the method of presentation, from the intrinsic value of the object to its value as a form, from the austerity of truth and the inflexible demands of morality to the relaxing harmony of beauty. This will happen more or less consistently, and more or less consciously, until everything terminates finally in a frame of mind which no longer recognizes intrinsic truth, with its severe "thus and not otherwise," nor the moral idea with its unconditional "either—or," but which seeks for significance in form and expression alone. That which is objective, whether it is a natural object, a historical event, a man, a sorrow, a preference, a work, a legal transaction, knowledge, an idea, is merely viewed as a fact without significance. It serves as a pretext for expression, that is all.[2] Thus originates the shadowy image of absolute form, a manner without a matter, a radiance without heat, a fact without force.[3]

---

[2] Oscar Wilde's "Intentions" are quite clear on this point.

[3] The writer has been reproached with treating the subject too simply in this exposition. He has deliberately shortened it for the sake of the fundamental idea,

People who think like this have lost the ability to grasp the profundity of a work of art, and the standard by which to measure its greatness. They no longer comprehend it as being what it is, as a victory and as an avowal. They do not even do justice to the form which is the exclusive object of their preoccupation; for form means the expression of a substance, or the mode of life of an existent being.

Truth is the soul of beauty. People who do not understand what the one and the other are really worth turn their joyful play into mere empty trifling. There is something heroic in every great and genuine creation, in which the interior essence has won through opposition to its true expression. A good fight has been fought, in which some essential substance, conscious of the best elements within itself, has set aside that which is extraneous to itself, submitted all disorder and confusion to a strict discipline, and obeyed the laws of its own nature. A tremendous ebullition takes place, and an inner substance gives external testimony to its essence and to the essential message which it holds. But the aesthete looks upon all this as pointless trifling.

Nay, more. Aestheticism is profoundly shameless. All true beauty is modest. This word is not used in a superficial sense. It has no relation as to the suitability of this or that for utterance, portrayal, or existence. What it means is that all expression has been impelled by an interior urge, justified by immutable standards, and permitted, even offered existence by the latter. This permission and obligation, however, only reside in the intrinsic truth of an entity or a genuine spiritual experience. Expression on the other hand for the sake of expression, self-elected as both matter and form, has no longer any value.

and has neglected many of its ramifications which should actually have been discussed. Yet after careful testing he finds no reason for altering his method of procedure. In a profounder sense, that which he here says is nevertheless justified.

We are led yet further afield by these considerations. In spite of the most genuine impulse, and even when truth not only emphatically justifies the proceeding, but also imperatively demands it, all true inwardness still shrinks from self-revelation, just because it is full of all goodness. The desire for revelation, however, and the realization that it is only in articulation that it can obtain release from the tyranny of silence, compel the expression of an inwardness; yet it still shrinks from disclosure, because it fears that by this it will lose its noblest elements. The fulfillment of all inwardness lies in the instant when it discloses itself in a form appropriate to its nature. But it is immediately conscious of a painful reaction, of a sensation as of having irrevocably lost something inexpressibly precious.

This applies—or is it too sweeping a statement?—to all genuine creative art. It is like a blush after the word, readily enough spoken, but followed by a secret reproach, an often incomprehensible pain, arising from depths till now unexplored; it is like the quick compression of the lips which would give much to recall the hasty avowal. People who understand this are aware that further depths and modestly concealed riches still lie beyond that which, surrendering itself, has taken shape. This generosity, while at the same time the store remains undiminished, this advance, followed by withdrawal into resplendent fastnesses, this grappling with expression, triumphant expansion, and timid, dolorous contraction, together constitute the tenderest charm of beauty.

But all this—the restrained yet youthful fullness of candor vanishes before the glance, at once disrespectful and obtuse, of those who seek after articulation for the sake of articulation, and after beauty for the sake of beauty.

Those who aspire to a life of beauty must, in the first place, strive to be truthful and good. If a life is true it will automatically become beautiful, just as light shines forth when flame is kindled. But if they seek after beauty in the first place, it will fare with them as it fared with Hedda Gabler, and in the end everything will become nauseating and loathsome.

In the same way—however strange it may sound—the creative artist must not seek after beauty in the abstract, not, that is, if he understands that beauty is something more than a certain grace of external form and a pleasing and elegant effect. He must, on the contrary, with all his strength endeavor to become true and just in himself, to apprehend truth and to live in and by it, and in this way fully realize both the internal and external world. And then the artist, as the enemy of all vanity and showiness, must express truth as it should be expressed, without the alteration of a single stroke or trait. It follows that his work, if he is an artist at all, will, and not only will, but *must* be beautiful. If, however, he tries to avoid the toilsome path of truth, and to distill form from form, that which he represents is merely empty illusion.

People who have not enjoyed—repulsive word, which puts beauty on a par with a titbit, and originates from the worthless conception which we have just now censured—human perfection or the beauty of a work of art, but desire closer familiarity with it, must take the inner essence for their starting-point. They will be well advised to ignore expression and harmony of form at first, but to endeavor to penetrate instead to the inner truth of the vital essence. Viewed from this standpoint, the whole process by which the matter transposes itself into its form becomes apparent, and the spectators witness a miraculous flowering. This means that they are familiar with beauty, although perhaps they may not consciously recognize it for what it is, but are merely aware of a sentiment of perfect satisfaction at the visible and adequate fulfillment of an object or of an existence.

Beauty eludes those who pursue it for its own sake, and their life and work are ruined because they have sinned against the fundamental order of values. If a man, however, desires to live for truth alone, to be truthful in himself and to speak the truth, and if he keeps his soul open, beauty—in the shape of richness, purity, and vitality of form—will come to meet him, unsought and unexpected.

What profound penetration and insight was shown by Plato, the master of aesthetics, in his warnings against the dangers of excessive worship of beauty! We need a new artist-seer to convince the young people of our day, who bend the knee in idolatrous homage before art and beauty, what must be the fruit of such perversion of the highest spiritual laws.

We must now refer what has already been propounded to the liturgy. There is a danger that in the liturgical sphere as well aestheticism may spread; that the liturgy will first be the subject of general eulogy, then gradually its various treasures will be estimated at their aesthetic value, until finally the sacred beauty of the House of God comes to provide a delicate morsel for the connoisseur. Until, that is, the "house of prayer" becomes once more, in a different way, a "den of thieves." But for the sake of Him who dwells there and for that of our own souls, this must not be tolerated.

The Church has not built up the *Opus Dei* for the pleasure of forming beautiful symbols, choice language, and graceful, stately gestures, but she has done it—in so far as it is not completely devoted to the worship of God—for the sake of our desperate spiritual need. It is to give expression to the events of the Christian's inner life: the assimilation, through the Holy Ghost, of the life of the creature to the life of God in Christ; the actual and genuine rebirth of the creature into a new existence; the development and nourishment of this life, its stretching forth from God in the Blessed Sacrament and the means of grace, towards God in prayer and sacrifice; and all this in the continual mystic renewal of Christ's life in the course of the ecclesiastical year. The fulfillment of all these processes by the set forms of language, gesture, and instruments, their revelation, teaching, accomplishment and acceptance by the faithful, together constitute the liturgy. We see, then, that it is primarily concerned with reality, with the approach of a real creature to a real God, and with the profoundly real and serious matter of redemption. There is here no question of creating beauty, but of finding salvation for sin-stricken humanity. Here truth is at stake, and the fate of the soul, and real—yes, ultimately the only real—life. All this it is which must be revealed, expressed, sought after, found, and imparted by every possible means and method; and when this is accomplished, lo! it is turned into beauty.[4]

This is not a matter for amazement, since the principle here at work is the principle of truth and of mastery over form. The interior element has been expressed clearly and truthfully, the whole superabundance of life has found its utterance, and the fathomless profundities have been plainly mapped out. It is only to be expected that a gleam of the utmost splendor should shine forth at such a manifestation of truth.

For us, however, the liturgy must chiefly be regarded from the standpoint of salvation. We should steadfastly endeavor to convince ourselves of its truth and its importance in our lives. When we recite the prayers and psalms of the liturgy, we are to praise God, nothing more. When we assist at Holy Mass, we must know that we are close to the fount of all grace. When we are present at an ordination, the significance of the proceedings must lie for us in the fact that the grace of God has taken possession of a fragment of human life. We are not concerned here with the question of powerfully symbolic gestures, as if we were in a spiritual theater, but we have to see that our real souls should approach a little nearer to the

---

[4] The Abbot of Maria Laach rightly remarks in this connection, "I stress the point that the liturgy has *developed* into a work of art; it was not deliberately formed as such by the Church. The liturgy bore within itself so much of the seed of beauty that it was of itself bound to flower ultimately. But the internal principle which controlled the form of that flowering was the essence of Christianity." (Herwegen, "Das Kunstprinzip der Liturgie," p. 18, Paderborn, 1916.)

real God, for the sake of all our most personal, profoundly serious affairs.

For it is only thus that perception of liturgical beauty will be vouchsafed to us. It is only when we participate in liturgical action with the earnestness begotten of deep personal interest that we become aware why, and in what perfection, this vital essence is revealed. It is only when we premise the truth of the liturgy that our eyes are opened to its beauty.

The degree of perception varies, according to our aesthetic sensitiveness. Perhaps it will merely be a pleasant feeling of which we are not even particularly conscious, of the profound appropriateness of both language and actions for the expression of spiritual realities, a sensation of quiet spontaneity, a consciousness that everything is right and exactly as it should be. Then perhaps an offertory suddenly flashes in upon us, so that it gleams before us like a jewel. Or bit by bit the whole sweep of the Mass is revealed, just as from out the vanishing mist the peaks and summits and slopes of a mountain chain stand out in relief, shining and clear, so that we imagine we are looking at them for the first time. Or it may be that in the midst of prayer the soul will be pervaded by that gentle, blithe gladness which rises into sheer rapture. Or else the book will sink from our hands, while, penetrated with awe, we taste the meaning of utter and blissful tranquillity, conscious that the final and eternal verities which satisfy all longing have here found their perfect expression.

But these moments are fleeting, and we must be content to accept them as they come or are sent.

On the whole, however, and as far as everyday life is concerned, this precept holds good, "Seek first the kingdom of God and His justice, and all else shall be added to you"—all else, even the glorious experience of beauty.

The Primacy of the Logos
over the Ethos

The liturgy exhibits one peculiarity which strikes as very odd those natures in particular which are generously endowed with moral energy and earnestness—and that is its singular attitude towards the moral order.

People of the type instanced above chiefly regret one thing in the liturgy, that its moral system has few direct relations with everyday life. It does not offer any easily transposable motives, or ideas realizable at first hand, for the benefit of our daily conflicts and struggles. A certain isolation, a certain remoteness from actual life characterize it; it is celebrated in the somewhat sequestered sphere of spiritual things. A contrast exists between the study, the factory, and the laboratory of today, between the arena of public and social life and the Holy Places of solemn, divine worship, between the intensely practical tendency of our time, which is opposed to life by its wholly material force and acrid harshness, and the lofty, measured domain of liturgical conceptions and determination, with its clearness and elevation of form.

From this it follows that we cannot directly translate into action that which the liturgy offers us. There will always be a constant need, then, for methods of devotion which have their origin in a close connection with modern life, and for the popular devotions by which the Church meets the special demands and requirements of actual existence, and which, since they directly affect the soul, are immediately productive of practical results.[1] The liturgy, on the contrary, is primarily occupied in forming the fundamental Christian temper. By it man is to be induced to determine correctly his essential relation to God, and to put himself right in regard to reverence for God, love and faith, atonement and the desire for sacrifice. As a result of this spiritual disposition, it follows that when action is required of him he will do what is right.

The question, however, goes yet deeper. What is the position of the liturgy generally to the moral order? What is the quality of the relation in it of the will to knowledge, as of the value of truth to the value of goodness? Or, to put it in two words, what is the relation in it of the Logos to the Ethos? It will be necessary to go back somewhat in order to find the answer.

It is safe to affirm that the Middle Ages, in philosophy at least, answered the question as to the relation between these two fundamental principles by decisively ranking knowledge before will and the activity attendant upon the functioning of the latter. They gave the Logos precedence over the Ethos. That is proved by the way in which certain frequently discussed questions are answered,[2] and by the absolute priority which was assigned to the contemplative life over the active;[3] this stands out as the fundamental attitude of

---

[1] Both in this connection and in countless others we find demonstrated the absolute necessity of the extraliturgical forms of spiritual exercise, the Rosary, the Stations of the Cross, popular devotions, meditation, etc. There could be no greater mistake than the attempt to build up liturgical life on an exclusively liturgical model. And it is equally mistaken merely to tolerate the other forms, because the "lower classes" need them, while setting the liturgy as the only possible pattern and guide before struggling humanity. Both are necessary. The one complements the other. Pride of place, however, belongs of course to the liturgy, because it is the official prayer of the Church. (Cf. my book, "Der Kreuzweg unseres Herrn und Heilandes," Introduction, Mainz, 1921.)

[2] Cf. the discussions on the significance of theology as to whether it is a "pure" science or one with an aim, that of bettering humanity; upon the essence of eternal happiness, whether it ultimately consists in the contemplation of God or in the love of Him; on the dependence of the will upon knowledge, and so on.

[3] It is significant that it was not until the seventeenth century, and then in the

the Middle Ages, which took the Hereafter as the constant and exclusive goal of all earthly striving.

Modern times brought about a great change. The great objective institutions of the Middle Ages—class solidarity, the municipalities, the Empire—broke up. The power of the Church was no longer, as formerly, absolute and temporal. In every direction individualism became more strongly pronounced and independent. This development was chiefly responsible for the growth of scientific criticism, and in a special manner the criticism of knowledge itself. The inquiry into the essence of knowledge, which formally followed a constructive method, now assumes, as a result of the profound spiritual changes which have taken place, its characteristic critical form. Knowledge itself becomes questionable, and as a result the center of gravity and the fulcrum of the spiritual life gradually shifts from knowledge to the will. The actions of the independent individual become increasingly important. In this way active life forces its way before the contemplative, the will before knowledge.

Even in science, which after all is essentially dependent upon knowledge, a peculiar significance is assigned to the will. In place of the former penetration of guaranteed truth, of tranquil assimilation and discussion, there now develops a restless investigation of obscure, questionable truth. Instead of explanation and assimilation, education tends increasingly towards independent investigation. The entire scientific sphere exhibits an enterprising and aggressive tendency. It develops into a powerful, restlessly productive, laboring community.

This importance of the will has been scientifically formulated in the most conclusive manner by Kant. He recognized, side by side with the order of perception, of the world of things, in which the understanding alone is competent, the order of practicality, of

face of universal opposition, that active Orders for women were founded. The history of the Order of the Visitation is especially instructive in this connection.

freedom, in which the will functions. Arising out of the postulations of the will he admits the growth of a third order, the order of
faith, as opposed to knowledge, the world of God and the soul.
While the understanding is of itself incapable of asserting anything on these latter matters, because it is unable to verify them by
the senses, it receives belief in their reality, and thus the final shaping of its conception of the world, from the postulations of the will
which cannot exist and function without these highest data from
which to proceed. This established the "primacy of the will." The
will, together with the scale of moral values peculiar to it, has taken
precedence of knowledge with its corresponding scale of values;
the Ethos has obtained the primacy over the Logos.

The ice having been broken, there now follows the entire course
of philosophic development which sets, in the place of the pure
will logically conceived by Kant, the psychological will, constitut-
ing the latter the unique rule of life—a development due to Fichte,
Schopenhauer, and von Hartmann—until it finds its clearest expression in Nietzsche. He proclaims the "will to power." For him,
truth is that which makes life sound and noble, leading humanity
further towards the goal of the "Superman."

Such is the origin of pragmatism, by which truth is no longer
viewed as an independent value in the case of a conception of the
universe or in spiritual matters, but as the expression of the fact
that a principle or a system benefits life and actual affairs, and
elevates the character and stability of the will.[4] Truth is fundamentally, if not entirely—though here we overstep the field marked out
for our consideration—a moral, though hardly a vital fact.

This predominance of the will and of the idea of its value gives
the present day its peculiar character. It is the reason for its restless

---

[4] This tendency has also influenced Catholic thought. A great deal of mod-
ernistic thought endeavors to make theological truth—dogma—dependent upon
Christian life and to estimate its importance not as a standard of truth, but as a
value in life.

pressing forward, the stringent limiting of its hours of labor, the precipitancy of its enjoyment; hence, too, the worship of success, of strength, of action; hence the striving after power, and generally the exaggerated opinion of the value of time, and the compulsion to exhaust oneself by activity till the end. This is the reason, too, why spiritual organizations such as the old contemplative orders, which formerly were automatically accepted by spiritual life everywhere and which were the darlings of the orthodox world, are not infrequently misunderstood even by Catholics, and have to be defended by their friends against the reproach of idle trifling. And if it is true that this attitude of mind has already become firmly established in Europe, whose culture is rooted in the distant past, it is doubly true where the New World is concerned. There it comes to light unconcealed and unalloyed. The practical will is everywhere the decisive factor, and the Ethos has complete precedence over the Logos, the active side of life over the contemplative.

What is the position of Catholicism in relation to this development? It must be premised that the best elements of every period and of every type of mind can and will find their fulfillment in this Religion, which is truly capable of being all things to all men. So it has been possible to adapt the tremendous development of power during the last five centuries in Catholic life, and to summon ever fresh aspects from its inexhaustible store. A long investigation would be needed if we were to point out how many highly valuable personalities, tendencies, activities and views have been called forth from Catholic life as a result of this responsiveness to the needs of all ages. But it must be pointed out that an extensive, biased, and lasting predominance of the will over knowledge is profoundly at variance with the Catholic spirit.

Protestantism presents, in its various forms, ranging from the strong tendency to the extreme of free speculation, the more or less Christian version of this spirit, and Kant has rightly been called its philosopher. It is a spirit which has step by step abandoned ob-

jective religious truth, and has increasingly tended to make conviction a matter of personal judgment, feeling, and experience. In
this way truth has fallen from the objective plane to the level of a
relative and fluctuating value. As a result, the will has been obliged
to assume the leadership. When the believer no longer possesses
any fundamental principles, but only an experience of faith as it
affects him personally, the one solid and recognizable fact is no
longer a body of dogma which can be handed on in tradition, but
the right action as a proof of the right spirit. In this connection
there can be no talk of spiritual metaphysics in the real sense of the
word. And when knowledge has nothing ultimately to seek in the
Above, the roots of the will and of feeling are in their turn loos-
ened from their adherence to knowledge. The relation with the supertemporal and eternal order is thereby broken. The believer no
longer stands in eternity, but in time, and eternity is merely connected with time through the medium of conviction, but not in a
direct manner. Religion becomes increasingly turned towards the
world, and cheerfully secular. It develops more and more into a
consecration of temporal human existence in its various aspects,
into a sanctification of earthly activity, of vocational labor, of communal and family life, and so on.

Everyone, however, who has debated these matters at any con-
siderable length clearly perceives the unwholesomeness of such a
conception of spiritual life, and the flagrance of its contradiction
of all fundamental spiritual principles. It is untrue, and therefore
contrary to Nature in the deepest sense of the word. Here is the real
source of the terrible misery of our day. It has perverted the sacred
order of Nature. It was Goethe who really shook the latter when he
made the doubting Faust write, not "In the beginning was the Word,"
but "In the beginning was the Deed."

While life's center of gravity was shifting from the Logos to
the Ethos, life itself was growing increasingly unrestrained. Man's
will was required to be responsible for him. Only one Will can do

this, and that is creative in the absolute sense of the word, i.e., it is the Divine Will.[5] Man, then, was endowed with a quality which presumes that he is God. And since he is not, he develops a spiritual cramp, a kind of weak fit of violence, which takes effect often in a tragic, and sometimes (in the case of lesser minds) even a ludicrous manner. This presumption is guilty of having put modern man into the position of a blind person groping his way in the dark, because the fundamental force upon which it has based life—the will—is blind. The will can function and produce, but cannot see. From this is derived the restlessness which nowhere finds tranquillity. Nothing is left, nothing stands firm, everything alters, life is in continual flux; it is a constant struggle, search, and wandering.

Catholicism opposes this attitude with all its strength. The Church forgives everything more readily than an attack on truth. She knows that if a man falls, but leaves truth unimpaired, he will find his way back again. But if he attacks the vital principle, then the sacred order of life is demolished. Moreover, the Church has constantly viewed with the deepest distrust every ethical conception of truth and of dogma. Any attempt to base the truth of a dogma merely on its practical value is essentially un-Catholic.[6] The Church represents truth—dogma—as an absolute fact, based upon itself, independent of all confirmation from the moral or even from the practical sphere. Truth is truth because it is truth. The attitude of the will to it, and its action towards it, is of itself a matter of indif-

[5] Yet even here reason affirms that God is not merely an Absolute Will, but, at the same time, truth and goodness. Revelation seals this, as it does every form of spiritual perception, by showing us that in the Blessed Trinity the "first thing" is the begetting of the Son through the recognition of the Father, and the "second" (according to thought, of course, not according to time) is the breathing forth of the Holy Ghost through the love of Both.

[6] Here nothing is said, of course, against the endeavor to exhibit the value of dogma in the abstract, and that of the single dogmatic truth for life. On the contrary, this can never be done forcibly enough.

ference to truth. The will is not required to prove truth, nor is the latter obliged to give an account of itself to the will, but the will has to acknowledge itself as perfectly incompetent before truth. It does not create the latter, but it finds it. The will has to admit that it is blind and needs the light, the leadership, and the organizing formative power of truth. It must admit as a fundamental principle the primacy of knowledge over the will, of the Logos over the Ethos.[7]

This "primacy" has been misunderstood. It is not a question of a priority of value or of merit. Nor is there any suggestion that knowledge is more important than action in human life. Still less does a desire exist to direct people as to the advisability of setting about their affairs with prayer or with action. The one is just as valuable and meritorious as the other. It is partly a question of disposition; the tone of a man's life will accentuate either knowledge or action; and the one type of disposition is worth as much as the other. The "Primacy" is far rather a matter of culture—philosophy, and indeed it consists of the question as to which value in the whole of culture and of human life the leadership will be assigned, and which therefore will determine the decisive tendency; it is a precedence of order, therefore, of leadership, not of merit, significance, or even of frequency.

But if we concern ourselves further with the question, the idea occurs that the conception of the Primacy of the Logos over the Ethos could not be the final one. Perhaps it should be put thus: in life as a whole, precedence does not belong to action, but to existence. What ultimately matters is not activity, but development. The roots of and the perfection of everything lie, not in time, but in eternity. Finally, not the moral, but the metaphysical conception of

---

[7] This is said of knowledge, not of comprehension; of the primacy of knowledge over the practical, of the contemplative over the active life, in the way understood by the Middle Ages, even if it lacks the latter's cultural-historical characteristics. On the other hand, it is impossible for us to free ourselves sufficiently from the domination of pure comprehension, as it has endured for half a century.

the world is binding, not the worth-judgment, but the import-judgment, not struggle, but worship.

These trains of thought, however, trespass beyond the limits of this little book. The further question—if a final precedence must not be allotted to love—seems to be linked with a different chain of thought. Its solution perhaps lies within the possibilities we have already discussed. When one knows, for instance, that for a time truth is the decisive standard, it is still not quite established whether truth insists upon love or upon frigid majesty; the Ethos can be an obligation of the law, as with Kant, or the obligation of creative love. And even face to face with existence it is still an open question whether this obligation is a final rigid inevitability, or if it is love transcending all measure, in which the impossible itself becomes possible, to which hope can appeal against all hope. That is what is meant by the question whether love is not the greatest of these. Indeed, it is. Nothing less than this was announced by the "good tidings."

In this sense, too, as far as the primacy of truth—but "truth in love"—is concerned, the present question is to be resolved.

As soon as this is done the foundation of spiritual health is established. For the soul needs absolutely firm ground on which to stand. It needs a support by which it can raise itself, a sure external point beyond itself, and that can only be supplied by truth. The knowledge of pure truth is the fundamental factor of spiritual emancipation. "The truth shall make you free."[8] The soul needs that spiritual relaxation in which the convulsions of the will are stilled, the restlessness of struggle quietened, and the shrieking of desire silenced; and that is fundamentally and primarily the act of intention by which thought perceives truth, and the spirit is silent before its splendid majesty.

In dogma, the fact of absolute truth, inflexible and eternal, en-

---

[8] John viii. 32.

tirely independent of a basis of practicality, we possess something
which is inexpressibly great. When the soul becomes aware of it, it
is overcome by a sensation as of having touched the mystic guar-
antee of universal sanity; it perceives dogma as the guardian of all
existence, actually and really the rock upon which the universe
rests. "In the beginning was the Word"—the Logos. . . .

For this reason the basis of all genuine and healthy life is a
contemplative one. No matter how great the energy of the volition
and action and striving may be, it must rest on the tranquil contemplation of eternal, unchangeable truth. This attitude is rooted in
eternity. It is peaceful, it has that interior restraint which is a victory over life. It is not in a hurry, but has time. It can afford to wait
and to develop.

This spiritual attitude is really Catholic. And if it is also a fact,
as some maintain, that Catholicism is in many aspects, as com-
pared with the other denominations, "backward," by all means let
it be. Catholicism could not join in the furious pursuit of the un-
chained will, torn from its fixed and eternal order. But it has in
exchange preserved something that is irreplaceably precious, for
which, if it were to recognize it, the non-Catholic spiritual world
would willingly exchange all that it has; and this is the primacy of
the Logos over the Ethos, and by this, harmony with the established and immutable laws of all existence.

Although as yet the liturgy has not been specifically mentioned,
everything which has been said applies to it. In the liturgy the Logos
has been assigned its fitting precedence over the will.[9] Hence the
wonderful power of relaxation proper to the liturgy, and its deep
reposefulness. Hence its apparent consummation entirely in the
contemplation, adoration and glorification of Divine Truth. This is
also the explanation of the fact that the liturgy is apparently so
little disturbed by the petty troubles and needs of everyday life. It

[9] Because it reposes upon existence, upon the essential, and even upon existence in love, as I hope to be able to demonstrate upon a future occasion.

also accounts for the comparative rareness of its attempts at direct teaching and direct inculcation of virtue. The liturgy has something in itself reminiscent of the stars, of their eternally fixed and even course, of their inflexible order, of their profound silence, and of the infinite space in which they are poised. It is only in appearance, however, that the liturgy is so detached and untroubled by the actions and strivings and moral position of men. For in reality it knows that those who live by it will be true and spiritually sound, and at peace to the depths of their being; and that when they leave its sacred confines to enter life they will be men of courage.

ALSO IN THE SERIES

Karl Adam
THE SPIRIT OF CATHOLICISM
Introduction by Robert A. Krieg

A brilliant and widely-influential reflection on the fundamental
nature of the Catholic faith and the Catholic Church.

Yves Congar
I BELIEVE IN THE HOLY SPIRIT

A major treatise on the Holy Spirit by one
of the great theologians of the century.

Support your local bookstore or order directly from the publisher at
www.CrossroadPublishing.com

To request a catalog or inquire about quantity orders, please e-mail
sales@CrossroadPublishing.com

We hope you enjoyed THE SPIRIT OF THE LITURGY.
Thank you for reading it.

crossroad
herder